DOGGED

BY ANDREA JAMES
& CATHERINE RYAN

CURRENCY PRESS
The performing arts publisher

GRIFFIN
THEATRE
COMPANY

CURRENT THEATRE SERIES

First published in 2021
by Currency Press Pty Ltd,
PO Box 2287, Strawberry Hills, NSW, 2012, Australia
enquiries@currency.com.au
www.currency.com.au
in association with Griffin Theatre Company

Typeset by Dean Nottle for Currency Press.
Cover photo by Brett Boardman, design by Alphabet.
Cover features Sandy Greenwood.

A catalogue record for this
book is available from the
National Library of Australia

NATIONAL
LIBRARY
OF AUSTRALIA

Contents

DOGGED   1

Theatre Program at the end of the playtext

Currency Press acknowledges the Traditional Owners of the Country on which we live and work. We pay our respects to all Aboriginal and Torres Strait Islander Elders, past and present.

Dogged was first produced by Griffin Theatre Company at the SBW Stables Theatre, Sydney, on 30 April 2021, with the following cast:

WOMAN	Blazey Best
DINGO	Sandy Greenwood
DOG	Anthony Yangoyan

Director, Declan Greene
Associate Director, Danielle Micich
Movement Director, Kirk Page
Set Co-designer and Costume Designer, Renée Mulder
Set Co-designer and Mural Artist, Peter Waples-Crowe
Lighting Designer, Verity Hampson
Sound and Composition, Steve Toulmin
Stage Manager, Ella Griffin
Assitant Stage Manager, Nicola Stavar
Associate Mural Artist, Jessica Johnson

ACKNOWLEDGMENTS

Acknowledgments for their invaluable inspiration, encouragement and assistance in this project's research and writing (in chronological order):

Peter Matheson; Ron Murray (Wemba Wemba); The Artists at the Malthouse Theatre and in Creative Development—Marion Potts, Van Badham, Paul Jackson, Matt Lutton, Jo Porter, Jason Tamiru, Anne-Louise Sarks, Josh Price, Nikki Shiels, Christina Smith; Lyn Watson and volunteers at the Dingo Discovery Centre, Toolern Vale; Deborah Bird Rose, *Wild Dog Dreaming* (2011), especially for her question 'What if the Angel of History were a Dog?', and for *Dingo Makes Us Human*, 1992, and for personally sharing her essay 'Death and Grief in a World of Kin' (2012), with our project; The Ngarinman, Ngaliwurru, Karangpurru, Bilinara, Wardaman, Mudbara, Gurindi, Malngin and Nyining knowledge holders from communities of Yarralin and Lingara who were Deborah Bird Rose's teachers; Alison and Jeff Burston; Joan Condon; My Anonymous Dogman; Uncle Rick Nelson (Dja Dja Wurrung); Tamsin Whaley; Toby Channing; Tandy Annuscheit (Taungurung); Shiralee Hood (Kurnai); Andrea James (Yorta Yorta/Gunaikurnai); Karen Berger; Zsuzsi Soboslay; Arian Wallach; Linda van Bommell; Donna Haraway, *When Species Meet*, (2008); Val Plumwood, *Nature in the Active Voice* (2012) and *Being Prey* (2000); Anna Krien, 'Us and Them'*, Quarterly Essay 45*, (2012); Walter Benjamin, *Theses on the Philosophy of History VII*; Eliza Hutchison; Bill Gammage, *The Biggest Estate on Earth*, (2011); Deirdre Slattery; Playwriting Australia and the 2017 National Script Workshop Team—Tim Roseman, Iain Sinclair, Michelle Kotevski, Uncle Max Harrison (Yuin); Andrea James (Yorta Yorta/Gunaikurnai), Phoebe Grainer (Kuku Djungan), Taylor Ferguson, Leila Enright, Jorjia Gillis (Budawang/Yuin), Will Hall; *The Dingo Debate: Origins, Behaviour and Conservation*, (2015), edited by Bradley Smith; *The Dogs That Made Australia* (2018) by Guy Hull; Aunty Glenys Watts (Gunaikurnai);Tim Paton (Gunaikurnai); Gratten Mullet (Gunaikurnai); Jill Redwood; Kerry Seaton; George Seddon, *Searching for the Snowy: An environmental history* (1994); Cal Flyn, *Thicker Than Water* (2016);

Phillip Pepper with Tess De Araugo, *The Kurnai of Gippsland* (1985); the 2019 PWA Lost Plays workshop team—Michelle Kotevski, Peter Matheson, Kate Gaul, Phoebe Grainer (Kuku Dungan), Peta Brady, Lincoln Vickery, Megan Wilding (Gamilaroi), Lucille MacKellar; the Griffin Theatre 2021 production team—Declan Greene, Sandy Greenwood (Gumbaynggirr, Dunghutti and Bundjalung), Blazey Best, Anthony Yangoyan.

And, as always, Daydd Kelly, Xanthe Ryan and Lucy-the-dog and Arnum Endean and Erik-the-dog. And, most importantly all the dingoes and dogs met along the way, for their constant presence, teaching and encouragement throughout this whole process and the miracle of Wandi the pup who dropped from the sky.

This playscript was created on the Countries of the Jaara Jaara, Gadigal and Darkinjung peoples. We acknowledge their ongoing culture and care of country and their Elders past, present and future.

Andrea James and Catherine Ryan

Dedication

Catherine began this project years ago with special dedication to the memory of her friend and colleague Leverne McDonnell, her friendship with animals and her belief in theatre.

FUNDING AND SUPPORT ACKNOWLEDGEMENTS:

Dogged was originally commissioned by Malthouse Theatre, Marion Potts Artistic Director. This project has been assisted by the Australian Government through the Australia Council for the Arts, its arts funding and advisory body. This project is supported by the Victorian Government through Creative Victoria. *Dogged* was developed with the support of Playwriting Australia through the National Script Workshop (2017), the Duologue (2018) and the Lost Plays (2019) Programs.

The project was helped with a Regional Arts Fund Quick Response Grant. The Australian Government's Regional Arts Fund is provided through Regional Arts Australia, administered in Victoria by Regional Arts Victoria. Castlemaine State Festival's She-d Residency Program assisted in the development of *Dogged*.

CHARACTERS

DINGO: All-seeing and all-knowing across time and place. Real and unreal. Mystical and earthly. Starving and grieving her lost mate and litter of three pups; she is protective, nurturing, fearsome and wily. Dexterous and supremely clever, she can twist and bend herself out of most tricky situations. Bound to this earth, her very survival depends on running with her lost pack.

WOMAN: Heading into her 40s. Daughter of a white farming family.

DOG: Woman's family's male dog. Their favourite working dog, who gets some special attention, including indoors time. A loving, energetic kelpie. Domesticated, loyal, dependent, compliant, eager for companionship, with a strong desire to please.

KILLER DOG LOST: A hybrid, purpose-bred hunting dog who has been abandoned in the mountains by his abusing humans. He is desperate, explosive, and reactionary. Lost, frightened, confused, he moves on all fours, low to the ground. Programmed to blood lust by the hunter, yet he is terrified and overwhelmed to be released from his prison-cage into the complexity of the forest.

PUP: A dingo pup. An exquisite lifelike life-sized puppet operated by one or more puppeteers from the cast. Weary and self-protective, her survival instinct is set to maximum.

Cast of three:

DINGO

WOMAN

DOG / KILLER DOG LOST

(PUPPET PUP)

SETTING

Gunaikurnai Mountain Country—noting that this scenario plays out in its own ways in Countries all across Australia.

TIME

An everpresent boundless immediate now.

DIVERSITY STATEMENT—The Create Diversity Pledge

We encourage the producer to collaborate with artists from diverse backgrounds in the realisation and presentation of this work. The Dingo character must be played by an Australian Indigenous Woman so that the connections to Country and People resonate on many levels.

TEXTUAL NOTES

When a / appears in the dialogue, it indicates a point of vocal overlap or unison. For example:

DINGO: My strength will return and I'll be / off
DOG: Rffff!
WOMAN: Hello, old boy.

This play text went to press before the end of rehearsals and may differ from the play as performed.

PRELUDE / AUDIENCE ENTRY

From the foyer, the audience enter into a completely darkened space, filled with summer night sounds of the Gunaikurnai bush. The audience should be shown to their seats by torchlight. It takes some time until the audience have fully transitioned into this dark world, and are immersed. Any theatre pre-show announcements should happen in the foyer, prior to entry.

The sounds of heartbeats gather one by one, until there is a cacophony of heartbeat rhythms. When the entire audience is seated, the sound-scape begins to almost imperceptibly thin—particular sounds disappear one by one, leaving increasing aural space and the heartbeat of a lone agitated female.

SCENE ONE

Imperceptibly, the lights fade up to a dim level on the audience.

DINGO *emerges. She is emaciated, desperate, unpredictable and sometimes playful.*

DINGO: Pfft!
Pfft!
Ever feel like you're being watched?
Eyes in the bush.
A flicker.

A flash of yellow, or black or tan …
Was it …?
Did I just …?

> *She approaches the audience very cautiously, looking for food, always looking for an escape if need be.*

Do you have a snack?
A rabbit in your handbag?
A possum under your T-shirt?

Gotta get my strength up.

Find my little ones.

She jumps on the ledge and listens to the audience's heartbeats.

Boom boom. Boom boom. Boom boom.
I could hear your heartbeats from miles away.

I've been sussing you out. Who's weaning their young. The little pups. Watching your eyebrows move. Your noses twitch, a lick of the lips. How sharp your teeth are.

Or not!

The way your ears never move. Never.

What's with that?

Boom boom. Boom boom. Boom boom.

Where are the weaklings? Which one of you is gonna get left behind to shrivel under a tree and who's gonna lead the pack?

Who limps, who coughs. Who's got a weak heartbeat.

[*Faintly*] Boom boom. Boom boom. Boom … boom … boom … boom.

She locates a weakling in the audience and targets them.

Ahhhhh. It's you!
A cough here.

Coughing.

A sniffle there.

Sniffling.

Which one of you is the alpha?
Boom boom! Boom boom! Boom boom! Boom boom!

She locates the alpha in the audience pack. Sits next to them.

Grrrrrrr.
Settle down there.
Settle down.

Have you seen my pups?!

My little ones?
Two boys and a girl?

I swear to Dog, I'll rip your throat out!

She paws at her painful teats.

Swollen teats.
Milk's going hard.

I've been searching for days.
Weeks!

She sniffs the audience again.

[*Looking forward*] Do you have a sausage, a snack, a tidbit for an old girl?

Just leave it on the ground. I'll come back later.

Gotta build up my strength.

Find my little ones.

A gunshot peals out from the valley below.

Shit!

DINGO *takes cover and watches.*

SCENE TWO

WOMAN *fires off two gunshots from offstage and enters dragging two fresh wild dog carcasses along the ground.* DOG *jumps around her enthusiastically.*

WOMAN *makes two long slits with her knife from the dogs' nose to the tail and roughly skins them.*

WOMAN *hangs the skins to dry.*

DOG *sniffs around them.*

DOG *looks directly into the faces of the prey and recognizes something of himself in them—a fleeting disturbance.*

WOMAN *shoos him away and he obeys.*

DOG *observes quietly.*

DINGO: See how she takes their lives, these dogs?
Then takes their skins?

That thinnest strip is all the proof she wants.

And leaves the rest to waste.
No fucking respect.
Those dead dogs are calling me too.

These poor unloved mongrels.
Bitsa this and bitsa that.
WOMAN: Come over here, gorgeous.

> DOG *runs to her for certainty and comfort.*

DINGO: So hungry.

> WOMAN *gives* DOG *a cuddle.*

> DINGO *disappears.*

WOMAN: Right.
Time for some afternoon tea. Mum's fruitcake.

> WOMAN *puts a billy on the fire, gets her lunchbox from her pack and wipes her forehead, accidentally smearing blood from her hand.*

Fuck!

> WOMAN *hastily wipes the blood off her forehead, then eats.*

> DOG *watches hungry and keen on the cake.*

> WOMAN *returns to the carcasses and rips out some entrails for* DOG.

Here's a treat then,
For your good work.
Another bloody day at the office.
Have a go at those, boy …

> WOMAN *resumes her afternoon tea.*

> *They both look in silence at the scene of carnage before them. It is slightly unsettling.*

> DINGO *reappears, closer.*

> WOMAN *is oblivious.*

> DOG *looks around him, sensing* DINGO*'s presence and movement. He is on the alert.*

> *Some time passes.*

WOMAN *settles, breathes out deeply.*

DINGO: Food.

DOG: Grrr …

WOMAN: You hearing something, Dog?

What's wrong?

Someone there?

WOMAN *tries to see into the bush. She looks for her gun, but realises it is metres away.* WOMAN *cannot understand what* DINGO *is saying.*

DOG: Grrr …

WOMAN: Undergrowth's so thick,

Sun's flaring and the shadows are all wrong.

I can't see a thing.

DINGO: Ha!

You can't, silly bitch.

But I can.

DOG: Grrr …

WOMAN: What is it?

DINGO: Watching.

Waiting.

Let them feel it …

DOG: Grrr …

WOMAN: One of us has got to move

and it's not going to be me.

DINGO: Just back slowly away.

WOMAN *reaches for her gun, while keeping eyes on* DINGO*'s spot.*

Boom boom …

WOMAN *holds her gun towards* DINGO*'s spot.*

DOG: Grrrrrrrrrr!

WOMAN: Shut up, Dog! Settle!

There is a stand-off, both waiting for the other to be lured out …

WOMAN *pulls out some wild dog entrails from a carcass, while holding her gun. Places them on the ground a short distance from* DINGO*'s spot.*

DOG *wants it.* WOMAN *shoos him away.*

DINGO: Good.

So so hungry.

Wait.

DOG: Grrr.

WOMAN: Stay, Dog.

DINGO: Think. Act. Survive.

Watch me bite the hand that feeds me.

Charged silence until ...

... the foliage moves.

WOMAN *holds her aim.*

DOG: Rrrrruff!

WOMAN: Wo!

Come on out, you coward!

Get outta there!

Let us get a good look at you before I shoot!

DOG: Rrrrufffff! Rrrruufffff! Grrrrrrr! /

WOMAN: Easy, boy.

WOMAN *and* DINGO *stand their ground until ...*

DINGO *allows herself to be seen.*

Fuck! It's a fucking dingo?!

DOG: Grrrrr. Woof! Woof! Woof! Woof! Woof! Woof! Woof!

WOMAN: Easy now.

DINGO: Stand my ground.

WOMAN: A pure fucking dingo?!

DOG: Grrrrr.

WOMAN: My old man told me about you ... Jesus. You're ...

She's awestruck and cannot find the words.

WOMAN *holds her aim at* DINGO, *sets her sight and holds* DOG *back with one hand by the collar.*

DOG: Grrrr.

WOMAN: Sit down.

Sit!

DINGO: Stand my ground.

DINGO *locks eyes with* WOMAN. DOG *falls silent as if smothered by a low-flying cloud.*

WOMAN: Fuuuuuck! A Bastard Wild Dog would run … or go me crazy, but …

DINGO: We travel in packs. Family units.

WOMAN: … not moving, just looking. Just like Dad said …
Meet one, and you will never forget.

> DINGO *is confident and strategic. She toys with* WOMAN'*s incredulity and surprise, asserting her presence as a warning.*

Dingo? … Or dog?

DINGO: Don't call me a fucking dog!
I am pure nature. Pure as the driven snow.

> DINGO *takes entrails and eats them hungrily, eyes fixed on* WOMAN *and* DOG *as she does.*

My strength will return and I'll be / off.

DOG: Rffff!

WOMAN: Hello, old boy.

DINGO: Don't call me 'old'! Or a 'boy'!

WOMAN: Fucking beautiful.

DOG: Rffff!

DINGO: [*talking and eating hungrily*] I could take you down if I wanted to. Me and my pack … We could take you down, no worries. We attack from the rear and kill. Via the throat. Mind you, we wouldn't do that unless we were hungry … Unless we were really hungry … Unless you fucked up my pack and my hunting ground … With ya dogs and ya foxes and ya deer and ya guns.

DOG: Grrrr!

WOMAN: Fucking beautiful.

> DINGO *holds* WOMAN'*s gaze.*

DINGO: Yes. I am.
And nearly dead for starving and missing my pups.
Watch me play the cute card.

> DINGO *puts on a cute face, cocks her head from side to side. She and* DOG *laugh.*

WOMAN: Oh, look!

How cute!

You are a beautiful one.

You want some more food?

DINGO *makes more cute face.*

Come on now.

You don't want to starve to death!

DINGO: Why do you care?

WOMAN: I'll put the gun over here, see?

WOMAN *makes a big show of putting the gun out of arm's reach.*

DINGO: I see it. I see it alright …

WOMAN: Here ya go, fella.

DINGO: Don't call me 'fella'.

WOMAN *gets more entrails from the carcass, holds them.*

DOG *whimpers.*

So fucking hungry.

DINGO *hesitates. Shivers.*

WOMAN: Look at you! You're freezing …

DINGO: Gotta find my pups …

DINGO *backs back.*

WOMAN: It's okay.

WOMAN *steps towards* DINGO, *puts the entrails on the ground.*

DINGO *steps back.*

I'll just leave the food here … Me and Dog will leave you alone now …

We'll just be over here. We're not looking.

DINGO *approaches the food.*

We're not looking. Are we, Dog?

DINGO *cautiously drags the food into the shadows and eats voraciously.*

WOMAN *sneaks some looks over her shoulder.*

Poor little fella.

DINGO *has finished her food and is waiting for more.*

Hasn't even hit the sides.

DINGO: Gotta get my strength up.

WOMAN: Let me look at you.

DOG *and* DINGO *circle and* DOG *sniffs* DINGO*'s arse.*

DINGO: Grrrrr!

WOMAN: Don't frighten him now.

DOG *starts dry humping the air.*

DINGO: Grrrrr!

WOMAN: Get away, Dog! Leave him be!

DOG *obeys, disappointed. Comes to* WOMAN*'s side.*

Oh, you are gorgeous.

Hey, look Dog! Dingo's not a boy! He's got teats!

DOG: Hmmph?

WOMAN: Awwwww. Where's your babies?

DINGO: Exactly. Where are they?

WOMAN: See, Dog! She likes us.

She's a girl.

DINGO: Don't call me 'girl'—

WOMAN: She really likes us.

DINGO *licks her paws. Her hunger sated.*

Dingo wants a pat? Look, Dog, Dingo wants a pat.

WOMAN *steps closer to* DINGO *and puts her hand to pat her.*

DINGO: [*baring her teeth and snarling*] Grrrr!

WOMAN: Okay. Okay! I won't hurt you.

Are you cold?

You could come over to the fire …

WOMAN *stokes the embers, flames slowly rise.* WOMAN *feeds the fire with more sticks.*

WOMAN *moves her gun closer to the fire, just in case she needs it …*

DINGO *watches, weighing up her next move.*

DOG *curls up at* WOMAN*'s feet.*

WOMAN *gently plays her harmonica—an old tune she remembers from her childhood.*

DOG *joins the song with soft howls. Snuggles into* WOMAN.

DINGO *enjoys the warmth of the fire, but stays on guard.*

WOMAN *looks at* DINGO.

Remember what Nan would say? About the dingoes?

Don't give me ya Bambi Big Eyes, she'd say.

You can fool the city idiots, she'd say,
but you can't fool me.

Fucking crazy killer scum scourge.

Like Monday night …

The lambs …

And Wednesday …
The ewes,
with half-born babies, faces ripped off hanging out their bloody mangled arses …

Poor old Dad fallen over in the mud
blubbering.
Been dragging their bodies
since before first light.

Load him onto the quad bike
drive home one-handed
holding onto him for dear life.
So many sheep killed,
him so broken.

Mum,
sitting quiet as at the kitchen table.
Her tea's gone cold
staring at Dad who's shaking, not eating, and the blood we couldn't
quite wash off him at the outside trough.
Wolf's at the door, Jeannie, wolf's at the door.
Over and over.

She's counting the sheep, doing the maths.
Checking again and again,
Lose too many more and we're going under,
Someone's got to stop them.

Like Nan said,
Only a matter of time till
they kill us too …

> WOMAN *pats* DOG.

> DOG *looks at* DINGO. *Uncertain. Suspicious.*

DINGO: We travelled in families
We travelled with the people
We were a team
Take down the big roos

Grab their hind legs
Two of us.
Then men spear 'em
Go back to camp
And we get a feed.

Run with the women too
Eat the possum scraps.
WOMAN: I'd trust you with my life.

> WOMAN *keeps patting* DOG.

DINGO: What's she doing to you?
DOG: I'm getting a pat.
DINGO: What?!
DOG: A pat!
DINGO: I'm here 'cause I'm hungry. Gotta get my strength back.
DOG: Mmm. Warm meat. My favourite.
DINGO: Find my pups.
DOG: Pups? Do you like the fire?
DINGO: Yeah.

> DOG *starts to pant.*

DOG: Warm, ay?

> DINGO *starts to pant.*

DINGO: Yeah … You do this every night?

DOG: Yep. They let me in. I get to lie by the pot belly on the farm.

DINGO: Pot belly? Like a beer gut?

DOG: No, the indoor fire. I'm the house dog. I look after the sheep.

DINGO: Good tucker.

DOG: What?!

DINGO: When we're desperate …

DOG: You look desperate to me!

DINGO: Gotta find my pups.

DOG: Yep, nothing like a pat and a feed and a warm fire.

DINGO: Every night?

DOG: Yeah! But they make me work for it though?

DINGO: Work?

DOG: Yep! Up at sparrow's fart. Running behind the quad bike.
'Hereya! Get up, Dog! Over here! Hereya! Not there, stupid!'

Rounding up sheep. Barking. Biting their arses. Jumping on their backs.

'Hereya! Get around! Get around!'

Crouch down. Ears forward. Sit. Run. Round up. Jump on bike.

Bloody hard work.

Then they feed you up. Sit you by the fire. Pat on the head and then out on the porch on the chain. Next day. Do it all over again.

DINGO: You let them chain you?!

DOG: Yeah …

DINGO: You don't hunt your own food?

DOG: Nope.

DINGO: Run through the bush?

DOG: Nope. Not on my own anyway.

DINGO: See the sunset from a cave?

DOG: Nope.

DINGO: Hang with your pack?

DOG: We're all chained up.

DINGO: Chained up?

DOG: Being out here is a bloody holiday!

DINGO: It's no bloody holiday here, mate.

This place is dangerous.

The other day, I was looking for a feed
with my pack.
Mum, Dad and the kids.

Beyond the piss marks,
comfort zone gone.
But we were starving.
Looking for food
anything will do.

And I'm tracking a lizard under the stones, my mate has got his
eyes on a skinny looking rabbit and the little ones are pouncing on
grasshoppers.

Yum yum yum.

And then it starts.

Bang!
They've got their sights on us.
Upwind.
I didn't smell a fucking thing.

Bang!
Mate for life goes down.
Noooooo!
And I yell to the little ones ...
Run!

Bang!
And we run!
Through the long grass.
In between the rocks.

Bang!
Sparks fly
and I yell to the little ones ...
Run!

Around the trees
and up that cliff there ...

Run!

My paws grab the rocks and I'm climbing,
cliff hanging!
Up and up and up and up!

Bang!
I pull myself up and over and look down …

Pause.

My mate lying there.
Blood pouring out of his ears and mouth.
No little ones.

Nothing. Just a smattering of blood on the sunlit rock.

A scuff.

There's a gunshot in the distance.

DINGO *pricks her ears.*

Have you seen my little ones?
DOG: Sorry …
DINGO: Two boys and a girl …
DOG: Sorry …
DINGO: Three roly-poly …
DOG: Nah …
DINGO: Two tan ones and one white like me …
DOG: Sorry …

DOG *and* DINGO *look to* WOMAN.

Hey, look! Girly's gone to sleep.
DINGO: Awwwwww! How cute!

DOG *snuggles up against her owner.*

What are you doing?!
DOG: Yep, gotta get in here now. Snuggle up … Keep warm.

WOMAN *hugs* DOG *in her sleep.*

Wanna join us?

A few gunshots in the distance. DINGO *stands to attention.*

WOMAN *stirs, but doesn't wake.*

DINGO: Shit. Gotta find my pups …

>   DINGO *goes to walk away.*

DOG: Hey! Where you going?

DINGO: I've gotta go.

DOG: Awesome! I'm coming too!
   Wait for me!

>   DINGO *exits.*

>   DOG *takes one final look at* WOMAN, *then to* DINGO, *back to* WOMAN, *and then exits too.*

SCENE THREE

DINGO *and* DOG *run 'slo-mo' into the early sunset, the landscape, trees and red clouds scrolling past like a vintage animation or children's toy.*

DINGO and DOG: [*together*] Yeeeeeeeeeehar!

DINGO: Over and under. Pads on soft warm earth. Let's go!

DOG: Yeah.

DINGO: Through the bushes. Scratch ya back.

DOG: Let's go!

DINGO: Twigs on face. Close your eyes. Push through. Eucalypt leaves gloss your feet, nostrils flare. Smells. Smells. Everywhere.

>   DOG *sniffing wildly.*

DOG: Oooh, yeah!

DINGO: Can you smell my pups?

DOG: Not yet.

DINGO: Let's go!
   Wind on your fur. Sun on your back.

DOG: Piss on this. Piss on that.

DINGO: Make your mark. Territory mine.

DOG: And mine!

DINGO: Not yet! Follow your nose. Follow the scent. Gotta find my pups. Down the hill.

DOG and DINGO: [*together*] Yeeeeehar!

DINGO: Through the puddles!

DOG: Mud! Mud!

DOG *splashes in mud.* DINGO *keeps running. Calling out to her pups.* DOG *is free.*

DINGO: Here, pups! Down, down, down the hill and up and up and … Wait!

There's a shadow on the ground. DINGO *freezes.* DOG *does too, but a little too late.*

A lamb carcass drops mysteriously from the sky.

DOG: What the—?!

DINGO: A dead thing.

DOG: Your pups?

DINGO: No. Thank Dog.

They approach the mangled lamb carcass

DOG: Oh … shit. It's a la …

/ Lamb!

DINGO: Lamb!

DINGO: Eagle got it.

DOG: [*looking up, cowering*] Old Flying Fox!

DINGO: Poor bubba lamb had the ride of its life.

DOG: A bird's-eye view.

DINGO: Eagle dropped its prey like a bit of dead meat. Ripped its guts out and left it here to rot. Eyes popped out of its head.

DOG: Guts ripped out.

DINGO: Maggots crawling.

DOG: Tail all squished.

DINGO: Baby fleece all brown and red and black and muddy.

DOG: Entrails spread out.

DINGO: Smells to high heaven.

Beat.

DINGO and DOG: [*together*] Let's roll in it!

DINGO *and* DOG *roll in the lamb carcass.*

DOG: / Yes … Oh God …

DINGO: / Oh yes … Sweet Jesus …

DOG: / Come to Mumma …

DINGO: / Ooohhh, that smells so good …

DINGO and DOG: [*together*] Mmmmm. Mmm-mmm.

> *Really working the stink into their backs and scent glands. When their work is done they both sit up and shake. Brown and black gunk is smeared on their necks and bodies.*

> *They smell a rabbit.*

DOG: It's a wabbit!

> DINGO *and* DOG *stalk the rabbit.* DOG *leads, making silent gestures as if he's a soldier in the field.* DOG *gestures to* DINGO *to lead,* DINGO *gestures 'No, after you'* ...

> DOG *takes up a Karate-Kid pose, stalks and then violently karate chops the rabbit to death to impress* DINGO.

DINGO: Wo! Way to go, Dog!

> DOG *snaps the rabbit in half with his teeth and gives some to* DINGO.

DOG: Yeah!

> DINGO *is impressed.*

DINGO: Come on! Gotta find my pups.
  This way.
  Scrambling rocks.
DOG: Boing! Boing!
DINGO: Around the trees.
DOG: Fresh green. Swish!
DINGO: A commando course. Traversed with ease.

> DOG *panting.*

  Slinking this way and that.
DOG: [*more panting, struggling to keep up*] Old ... charcoal ... logs ...
DINGO: Can you smell my pups?
DOG: Not yet.
DINGO: Hurry! Up!
  Running and running.
DOG: [*panting, but excited, out of control*] And running and running
  and ...
DINGO: Gotta go.
DOG: Soft earth.

DINGO: Becomes pebbles.
DOG: Becomes rocks.
   Ouch!
DINGO: Rock-hopping. Boing! Boing!
DOG: Scrambling.
   Ouch?!
   Wait!

> DINGO *helps* DOG *up.*

> DOG *pants, exhausted.* DINGO *sniffs, desperately searching for her pups.*

Where the fuck are we?
DINGO: Our den.

> DINGO *sniffs. It's empty.*

Nothing. No little ones.
DOG: Nothing?

> DINGO *howls. Calling out to her pack.*

DINGO: Owwwwwwwwwwwwww!
DOG: Cool!
DINGO: Owwwwwwwwwwwwww!
DOG: Owwww!

> DINGO *listens out for her pack. Nothing.*

DINGO: They're not here. Come on …
   Footprints in the dirt. Size ten chainsaw boots. Left a cigarette butt. Horizon. Pfft! A reward for a piss-weak day's work. Couldn't chase down a kill if he wanted to. Coward. You call yourself a hunter!
DOG: Hey! What's that?

> DOG *sniffs out a poisoned bait. A plastic yellow arrow points to the impending disaster below.*

DINGO: Don't touch that!
DOG: Why not?
DINGO: Stop!
DOG: Meat.
DINGO: Don't touch!
DOG: … Lip-smacking. Oh. My. God …

DINGO: Stop!

DOG: Heavenly meat!

DINGO: See that there. The yellow, pointing down?

DOG: Meat.

DINGO: Get a hold of yourself, Dog!

DOG: Mmmmeat.

DINGO: It's dingo bait, mate!

DOG: Mmmmmmmmeat!

DINGO: It'll taste good, alright. Too good to be true. Better than usual. And you'll scoff that limp flyblown meat / in one gulp. No need to chew.

DOG: / Mmmmmmmmmmmmmmmmmeat.

DINGO: Gulp! And there it lands inside your gut. Festering there. Letting go of its lethal weapon.

DOG: Love that movie! MMMMel!

DINGO: Dizzy. You'll feel dizzy at first. Fuzzy. Kinda nice. Squashed. Then the drool, running down your languid tongue. Salivating. Rivers of the stuff. Tongue on dirt resting in a pool of drool like a sad diving board.

And then the retching. You'll retch and retch and retch. Up she comes. But it's too late, the damage is done. Residue.

Then come the tremors. Convulsions that quake the earth. The pain. The pain. Eyes roll back. Breath like razor blades. In out. Shorter and shorter. Sharper and sharper. In out. Then out and out and out no more …

DOG: Bloody hell!

DINGO: Don't touch that! Do you hear me?!

DOG: Okay! Alright! I heard you!

DINGO: I told my pups never to touch that stuff!

DINGO *stands on alert. She hears* WOMAN*'s heartbeat.*

Boom boom. Boom boom.

DOG: What?

DINGO: I can hear her heartbeat.

Clapping away. Alive and living.
Warm meat.

Coming into my zone.
My territory!

WOMAN: [*calling from down below*] Doooo-og!

> DOG *and* DINGO *look out.*

DINGO: There she is!
Your what's-its-name …

> *Lights up on* WOMAN.

DOG: Owner?

WOMAN: Dooooo-og!

DINGO: I watch and wait.
Over boundless time.
Seasons change.
Pups are born.
And die again.

Watch and wait.

> DINGO *makes the sound of an angry heartbeat.*

Boom boom! Boom boom! Boom boom!

WOMAN: Dooooooog!

DOG: Shit! She sounds angry!

DINGO: Relaaax! Take a chill pill.

> *Lights focus on* WOMAN *now.*

WOMAN: Dooooo-og! Fucking Dog!

SCENE FOUR

At the cave.

DOG *stands up on his two legs and finds his swagger, desperately trying to keep* DINGO *impressed. They unite.*

WOMAN *hears* DOG's *words as sounds only, and does not comprehend them.*

DOG: Hey, Woman, wassup?

DINGO: Yeah, what he said …

WOMAN: [*gesturing to* DOG *to come to her heel*] Get down here!

DOG: Wad ya say?

WOMAN: Get here, now!

DINGO: Stand your ground.

WOMAN: Do-og!

DOG: Stand my ground.

> WOMAN *takes a step towards* DOG.

Grrrr!

DINGO: That-a-boy.

WOMAN: Dog?

> WOMAN *is afraid of* DOG *for an instant. She wraps the dog chain around her fist.*

DINGO: Stand your ground.

DOG: Stand my …

> WOMAN *charges towards* DOG *and takes control.*

WOMAN: Dog! Get here. Right now. Heel! Now.
Get!
Down!

> DOG *cowers and comes.*

DOG: Okay!

WOMAN: Now! Drop!

> DOG *drops at her feet and she grabs him by the collar.*

DINGO: What the—?

WOMAN: Never. Ever. Run away from me again! Have you got that?!
You'll go wild. Like this one here.

DINGO: Grrrr.

WOMAN: No! Don't do that ever again. I call. You come back.

> WOMAN *puts* DOG *on the (longish) chain.* DOG *whimpers.*

You frightened me!

> DOG *wags his tail.*

DOG: I'm sorry.

DINGO: Not sorry. No-one's sorry.

DOG: Please. Please. Pat me on the head. Scruff around the neck. Waggle waggle waggle. Big brown yes. Batting. Nuzzle on the leg.

WOMAN: Naughty Dog!

DOG whimpers and big-brown-eyes WOMAN.

Oh, alright! Come here then!

DOG jumps up and licks WOMAN *on the face.*

Phooooar! Go away! You stink! Both of you. You dirty rotten stinking …

DINGO: Death …

DOG: Dead things.

WOMAN: I just gave you a bath! Go away! The two of you! Go on! Get!

She kicks dust at DINGO *and sits herself away.*

Where are we?

DOG: Where are we?

DINGO: Hell's Pass.

DOG: Hell's Pass.

WOMAN: I've never been up this high before. Where's home?

DINGO: It's over there.

WOMAN: I can't see home. Shit! Now you've gone and got us lost.

DINGO: It's over there and my pups are nowhere to be seen.

WOMAN: Settle. Think. Gather my thoughts.

DINGO: It's over there.

> WOMAN *can't hear* DINGO, *looks out to the horizon.* DINGO *on the lookout for her pups.*

WOMAN: Wow. It's beautiful up here.

DOG: Let me see! Let me see! Whimper whimper.

WOMAN: I need to think. Need a rest. Need to wash my hands. Dirty rotten mongrel dog.

She washes her hands.

She sees DINGO.

You still here?! I said go away!

She throws a stick at DINGO *who scampers.*

You're lucky I don't have the energy …

DINGO: Too late.

> DINGO *jumps up onto the cave ledge, sniffs the air, still looking for her babies.*

WOMAN *collects wood to make a fire.*

DOG: Where are we?

DOG *strains on his chain.*

WOMAN: You're in the doghouse …
But geez, I'm glad you're back.

DINGO *starts to pace back and forth, back and forth, longing for her pups.*

I know this country like the back of my hand, Dog,
But I'm not feeling it like I used to, not these parts.
We had the run of it all when we were kids.
I can tell you who's who and what's where of all the families to great-, great-, great-grandparents back. Since Scotland and starvation …
All held in our bodies, familiar.
But
I've got no idea where I am anymore.

We'll stay the night, get our bearings with the morning sun.
And hunt our way back home.
Get back to Mum and Dad

A gunshot rings out. It's getting closer.

Wild dog hunters! Bloody blow-ins from the city. Another stinking boys' weekend killing party.

More gunshots across the valley. Echoing.

Shooting in the dark.
They must have spotlights.

Suddenly hundreds and hundreds and hundreds of moths flutter into the space. WOMAN *shoos them away.* DOG *snaps at them.*

DINGO: The moths!
WOMAN: / Ahhhh! What the—?!
DOG: / Grr. Ruff! Ruff!
WOMAN: There's hundreds of them! Get them off me!
DINGO: Beautiful. / My puppies loved the moths.
WOMAN: / It's on my face! Get it off me! Get it off me!
DOG: / Rrf! Rrf! Rrf! Rrf! Rrf!

DINGO: Magic.

WOMAN: They're huge! Fuck!
  They're everywhere!

  WOMAN *finally settles.*

Jesus.

  A moth lands on her hand. She lets it.

Eeewwwwww. It's on my hand. Will it bite me?

  She chuckles.

  It tickles.

  [*To the moth*] Hello. What are you doing up here?

DOG: Ruff! Ruff!

WOMAN: Leave him alone!

DINGO: Every year they come. Winging their way through the orange glow. Nine hundred miles or more. Wallpapering the caves. Good tucker. So they say.

  WOMAN *communes with the moth.*

DOG: Who say?

DINGO: The people. Pop them in the fire, singe the wings. Easy picking. So they say.

DOG: Who say?

DINGO: The people.

DOG: What people?

DINGO: Sleep, sleep, little ones, go to sleep. Rest now. Rest your weary wings.

DOG: Ruff! Ruff!

WOMAN: Shhh! Look! He's going to sleep.

DINGO: Sleep now in the cool dark space that Mother Earth has made just for you. Black as the blackest night. The blackest night that lasts forever. Sleep now, little ones. Land and sleep.

  The moth flies off WOMAN's *hand.*

WOMAN: There you go! Fly away, be free!

DOG: Grrr ruff!

  They watch the moth fly away.

WOMAN: Getting cold. Bloody cold. Bloody dogs!

DINGO: Mmm. Warm fire. Thank you.

WOMAN: What is this place? Where are we?

> *She looks out to the horizon.*

Fuck it's dark, can't see a thing.

DINGO: Goodnight, my puppies.

WOMAN: Mum and Dad will be wondering where I am. Where I got to. Cold.

> WOMAN *puts another log on the fire and the cave brightens. She makes a dog-shaped shadow on the wall with her hands.*

Grrr. Ruff! Ruff! Look, Dog!

> DOG *cocks his head from side to side.*

Look! It's you! Ruff! Rrruf!

DOG: Actually, that's really offensive.

WOMAN: Or what about you?

> *Signalling to* DINGO, *she opens up the mouth of a dingo shadow puppet and howls.*

Oowwwwwwwwwwwwww! / Oowwwwwwwwwwwwww!

DOG: / Don't. Please don't. You're embarrassing yourself.

> DINGO *and* DOG *cock their heads.* DOG *shivers over on the chain.*

Brrrrrrr! Brrrrrrr!

WOMAN: What's wrong, Dog? Someone left you out in the cold? Shoulda thought about that before you escaped into the wild.

> *She counts her skins.*

First light, we'll be off. And as for you …?

> *She looks at* DINGO *and then stares deep into the fire.*

DINGO: Warm. Warm fire. Warm bodies. My babies will be cold.

DOG: Brrr! Brrr! I'm freezing.

> WOMAN *relents and lets* DOG *off the chain.*

WOMAN: Come on then!

> DOG *snuggles up to* WOMAN. DINGO, *tentative at first, joins in the snuggle. She likes it.*

DINGO: See those lakes down there?

DOG: Where?

DINGO: I saw three men get turned into stone once.

> WOMAN *falls into a campfire reverie.*

DOG: What?!

DINGO: Long time now. At the camp.
We were waiting for the men to come back from the lakes.

DOG: We were?

DINGO: Us dingoes! With the women and children at the camp.
Good teamwork, see?
We'd been waiting all day. Waiting and watching.

The children are chattering, hungry now, waiting for their uncles and fathers to bring back a feed.

And then we saw them.

Us dingoes run to the shore and the women and children join us.

See the smoke?

DOG: Where?

DINGO: There's Yal Yal, Willambuleng and Cheeky, leaving smoke trails in their wake and using their 'gendooks' to push their canoes to shore …

We sniff at the men's fingers and they shoo us away!

'Shoo! Shoo!'

The women stoke the fires and the hungry children are crawling up their mother's legs.

We circle those men.

'Shoo! Shoo! Go on, get!'

And the women and children and us dingoes

We wait.

And wait. And wait. And wait.

And those women are getting wild.

Boom boom boom boom boom boom.

'Where's the fish?'

We can see the oil slick around the hunters' mouths and smell their fish-smelling fingers …

'Go on, get!'

And the women point and curse.

'What?! No fish? No fish for our children? No fish for our dingoes?'

They were wild!

Point and curse.

The earth rumbles and thunder booms.

The men cower and us dingoes run for cover.

Point and curse.

> *Beat.*

Those men?

They got turned into stone.

Frozen solid.

One. Two. Three.
DOG: Brrrrrrrr!
DINGO: For being greedy.
DOG: I'm not greedy!
DINGO: No you're not. But they are.

> DINGO*'s ears prick up. She hears an alpha's heartbeat.* DOG *senses it too.*

> *Torches flash, dogs bark and gunshots ring out.* DOG *barks.* DINGO *detects her pups' scent in the wind.*

WOMAN: The boys coming closer with their savage crossbreed dogs. Hungry for a kill. Those skins are mine.
DINGO: Wind's changed! I can smell my babies!

> DINGO *takes off.* DOG *bounds after her.*

> *More gunshots.*

WOMAN *stands, panicked.*

WOMAN: Dog? Wait! Don't leave me alone! Wait!

SCENE FIVE

DINGO *is on the scent trail of her pups.*

WOMAN *runs.*

DINGO: My little ones
    two boys and a girl
    three roly-poly.

    Two tan ones and one white one like me.

    Mummy's coming.

    Two gunshots, closer than before.

WOMAN: Doo-ogg!

    Gunshots echoing bouncing around
    Can't tell where they're coming from
    Or who?
    How many?
    And me, one woman.

    And her dog …

    Doo-ogg! Come back!

DINGO: Through the brush trees
    turn right
    then left

    right right then left and right again.

    Mummy's coming

WOMAN: Doo-ogg!

    Utefuls of them hunt in packs
    a fucking game
    and their dogs … shit, their dogs …

    And me, one woman …
    Alone.

DINGO: Feel the air getting lighter
   Feel the wind getting colder
   Feel the mist on my face and all around us.

   I can't see you
   But I can smell you, my little ones.

   Mummy's coming.
WOMAN: Dooo-oog! Don't leave me!
DINGO: Higher now.
WOMAN: Their booze their guns their keeping score …
DINGO: Wind whistles in our ears
   Eeeeeeeeeeeeeeeeeeee
   Exposed
   To the elements
   Laid bare.
WOMAN: Me alone.
   Afraid
   I know what you do …
   But you're not gonna stop me
   My kills my skins
   You're not gonna get them.
DINGO: I bound.
   I leap.
   I hold on tight.
   My babies.
   Mummy's coming.
WOMAN: Where are they?!
DINGO: I push myself up and over the rock face with my hind legs
   And—

>   DINGO *looks around at the denuded camp in the pre-dawn light
>   and sniffs at the remains of a crusty fire.*
>
>   WOMAN *looks around camp too.*

—Their camp.

Wild dog hunters.

Feral.

She sniffs at their spent campfire.

DOG *enters, panting.*

WOMAN: Dog!

DINGO: Styrofoam trays shrivelled and stinking in the ashes.

Meat, eating meat, while killing meat.

Beer cans.
Brown from the fire.

Breakfast of champions.

She sniffs some more.

Bullet cases,
empty now.

Too many to count.

WOMAN: Broken chain around tree.

DINGO: My babies?

DINGO *sniffs some more.*

WOMAN: Fat dog collar ripped, attached.

DINGO: Drunken tracks lead to piss puddles.
Limp dicks pissing golden streams.

WOMAN: State Dog Bounty for
beer money.
Pissing away your hundred bucks a skin.

DINGO: And they call us wild animals?

WOMAN: Shaking.
Sick with fear.

DINGO: Imprint of swags.
Three of them.

WOMAN: Where are they?

DINGO: Cigarette butts.
Suck that tar in
And—
Die, you fuckers!
Die!

Mummy's coming!

Chainsaw boot imprints
Size eleven and twelve.

Footprints.

DINGO *sniffs and follows the footprints snaking this way and that.*

Here, here, here, here, here, here and …
Here …

The golden sunset reveals a tree with fresh and dried skinned dingoes hanging from its branches.

Silence.
My family
My pack
My three little ones
and my mate for life.

Pause

Light spreads to slowly reveal many, maybe hundreds, of dog and dingo carcasses hanging down, in different stages of drying-out and decay.

WOMAN *and* DINGO *walk under the tree.* WOMAN *is dumbstruck, a bleached skull hangs perfectly positioned to meet her face to face.*

DINGO *turns on* WOMAN *and* DOG *and bares her teeth. A vision of matriarchal fury.*

Rrrrrrrrrrrrrrrraaaaar! You. Stupid. Fucking. Bitch.
WOMAN: Fuck! Shit! Get back, Dog!
DOG: Huh?

DINGO *lunges at* WOMAN.

DINGO: Rrrrrrrrrrrrrrrraaaaar!

Distorted sounds echo. Like a dingo howl played backwards. DINGO *faces* WOMAN *and looks her fair and square in the eyes. Hard.*

Holding DOG *back with one arm,* WOMAN *points her gun at* DINGO.

WOMAN: Get back! Get back, or I'll shoot!

DINGO: You fucking killer!.

WOMAN: Back!

DOG: Grrrrrr.

DINGO: I swear, I'll rip your fucking throat out!

WOMAN: Get back or I'll shoot.

> DINGO *shapeshifts and stands up on two legs, charges towards* WOMAN *who backs back back back.*

DINGO: Rrrrraaaaaar!

   Us dingoes … we walk on two legs, you know.

WOMAN: What are you doing?

DINGO: A dingo's balls are at the same place as a man's balls.

WOMAN: What?

DINGO: Kick him in the nuts, it hurts just the same.

   But I'm a bitch! Do you hear me?!

WOMAN: Yes! I can hear your words.

DINGO: What am I saying? Grrrr.

WOMAN: That … If … I don't know …

DINGO: What do you see?

WOMAN: Mist … Fog …

DINGO: Just like I thought.

   Now, fuck off! Leave me alone!

> WOMAN *is unresponsive. Still shocked and moved.*

SCENE SIX

DINGO *takes her babies and mate down from the hanging tree.*

She places them in a ritual circle.

WOMAN *and* DOG *are elsewhere in the space.* WOMAN *is oblivious to* DOG. DOG *slowly sickens.*

DINGO: No more running on this earth.

   We are but little pinpricks in the sky

   A puff of smoke.

   A wispy cloud.

   A figment.

WOMAN: Line upon line …

   Carcass upon carcass …

   Hanging from this Killing Tree

Hard
Dry.

Bleached
White
Skull.

Holes where its eyes had been
Bore into mine.
DINGO: A shadow of our former selves
An imprint
Bones and dust.
WOMAN: Head hangs down.
Same height as mine.
We meet.
Frozen.
We meet.
DINGO: A burnt brown fossilised stain on the cave floor
To be discovered a hundred years from now
Now you see me
Now you don't.
WOMAN: Line upon line of
Carcass upon carcass crowding
Like bark peeling from a forest of manna gums.
DINGO: Swinging now
Airborne
A morbid wind chime
Plays a torturous tune
From their twisted mouths …

'Gone Before Our Time …

    Beat.

We are 'Gone Before Our Time'.

    DOG *attempts to stand up on his two legs like* DINGO *too, but*
    falls. Stands. Falls.

WOMAN: Dog? Dog? What's wrong?
DOG: I'm sorry.
WOMAN: What?

DOG: I'm sorry.

WOMAN: I heard you …

I mean I actually heard you …

What you said …

This is crazy …

DOG: Back in that last gully.

It was the juiciest little sausage, I couldn't refuse.

The perfect mix of meat, filler, and …

WOMAN: No.

DOG: I'm sorry.

WOMAN: Oh God. No.

> DOG *stands and falls.* WOMAN *grabs him. Sounds warp, adding a discordant, dirge-like waltz, maybe with bits of harmonica, and warped variations on the earlier campfire song … They waltz awkwardly.*

DOG: Those bastards.

And the mountains and their creatures sing me a campfire funeral dirge.

Can you hear them?

A requiem,

For me and all the others.

> DINGO *sings her beautiful and haunting requiem. Harmonious howling.*

WOMAN: No.

DOG: Sausage plus poison, they sing.

Flour plus poison, they sing.

Waterholes plus poison, they sing.

You know, Girly.

You know how it goes,

How long this is going to take.

WOMAN: No.

DINGO: The pain.

WOMAN: Come on, chuck it up, we'll clean you out, we can …

DOG and DINGO: [*together*] It's too late.

WOMAN: No.

DINGO: You know what you have to do.

Pause.

DOG: Please.

> *The spinning ends.* DOG *retches. Shakes. Looks at his owner. Eyes pleading.*
>
> *Stillness.*

WOMAN: And slowly I polish my gun.

> *Pause.*

Check the ammunition.

DOG: Thank you.

WOMAN: Take aim,
Steady my shaking,
Take aim …

and …

DOG: My Girly …

> *Pause.*
>
> *Gunshot.*
>
> DOG *is killed. His spirit body exits, leaving his lifeless carcass on the ground.*
>
> *A silent glitter bomb explodes sending particles into the air. Boundaries continue to blur.* DINGO *and* WOMAN *speak from their own separate parts of the stage.*
>
> *Pause.*

DINGO: And then, what does the stupid bitch do?

WOMAN: Fuck off!

DINGO: She weeps.

> WOMAN *wills herself not to cry.*

WOMAN: Go away!

DINGO: Like I knew she would.

WOMAN: Get! You're just a dog! A wild dog! Stop talking to me!

> WOMAN *throws a stick.*

I said get!

DINGO: Too late.

WOMAN: Go away!

DINGO *lies with her dead family.*

WOMAN *cuddles her dead* DOG.

We lie together,
Me terrified, exhausted, clinging.
Sleeping forever.
Dreaming of a bed of a million moth wings.

WOMAN *grieves.*

Time passes.

DINGO *leaves her ritual space, and approaches* WOMAN.

DINGO: Aren't you gonna skin your dog now?
WOMAN: What?
DINGO: One hundred bucks right here. Just laying there in the dirt.

And you call yourself a *hunter.*

WOMAN *weighs up the situation.*

Staring at DINGO, *defiant, she skins* DOG.

She displays it to DINGO, *distressed, but strong. A challenge.*

Stares down DINGO.

WOMAN: Fuck you.

SCENE SEVEN

Suddenly from the bushes a wild KILLER DOG LOST *crashes through, barrelling straight towards* DINGO.

KILLER: Rooooaaarrrr!
DINGO: Fuck! Hunting dog!
KILLER: Freakin' out space freakin' out smells freakin' out sounds.
    Smells smells smells! Fucking blood!
    Volcano wild angry terrified high as a fuckin' …
    Hello, bitch, you're gorgeous.
    Fuckin' kite off my fuckin' face fuckin' gorgeous. Even if I wanted
    to I couldn't fuckin' help myself. Taste the blood …

WOMAN *is petrified, powerless in the chaotic movement.*

DINGO: Grrrr! Get away!

KILLER: Starved for days dropped in country I dunno whose.

Be my friend, go on please.

Master wants a kill wants a heart / smashing.

DINGO: Steady! Steady on, big fellow.

Grrrrrrr.

KILLER: country I don't know whose laws I couldn't give a fuck about and lets me loose to crash through.

Play? Please?

Freakin' out space.

Fuck you or kill you?

Freakin' out smells freakin' out sounds movement life.

DINGO: Who did this to my family?!

KILLER: Dave. And Adrian. And Mick.

DINGO: Grrrrrr.

> WOMAN *chills at the mention of the blokes. She looks around manically, on guard for them. Flips between being on her guard for the blokes somewhere off and* KILLER *in front of her.*

KILLER: They're top blokes. They shoot. I run. Grab the kill and bring it back.

'Good boy! That's a fulla! Good boy! Here, have some stinking meat.'

Mmmm.

Bang!

DINGO: Why?

KILLER: They shoot. I run and run and run and run.

Run and run and run and run

can't find the kill

can't find my blokes top / blokes

WOMAN: Blokes.

KILLER: Dave and / Adrian and Mick.

WOMAN: Shit shit shit.

KILLER: Have you seen my top blokes?

Doesn't matter now though, 'cause now I'm fucking free.

Fuckin' …

> KILLER *tries to mount* DINGO.

WOMAN *tries to get a sight on* KILLER *but it is too chaotic. She is panicked.*

DINGO: Nooo!

DINGO *snarls and rips a piece of flesh off* KILLER*'s flank. He squeals!*

KILLER: Ouch! You fucking bitch!

KILLER *lunges at* DINGO *with teeth bared. All snarls and vicious sounds.*

DINGO: I said *No!!!*

The horrifying sound of dogs snarling. Fur and blood flies through the air. An awful fight to the death. KILLER *has* DINGO *by the throat and is crushing her.*

KILLER: Now say sorry!

DINGO: No!

KILLER: Say … sorry or I'm gonna have to …

WOMAN: Get off her!

DINGO: … No …

KILLER: Come on, puppy wants a playmate …

DINGO: … No …

KILLER *is slowly squeezing the life out of* DINGO. *We see the whites of her eyes, breath getting shorter and shorter.*

WOMAN *fires a panicked shot into the air.*

WOMAN: Get off her! Get off her!
She's mourning her dead, for fuck's sake!
Let her be!

KILLER: Heart smashing rib cage wants to blast escape to smash explode bones blood / flesh self

DINGO *is awfully wounded and bleeding from the neck.*

A tight ball of violence.

WOMAN: Stop it!
Stop!

WOMAN *fires a panicked shot into the air.* KILLER *is squeezing the life out of* DINGO.

Stop!!!

> WOMAN *aims at* KILLER *and shoots again and hits* KILLER *in the shoulder.*
>
> *Finally,* KILLER *stops attacking* DINGO.

KILLER: Ouch!

> *Inexplicably, bagpipes play and* KILLER *starts dancing a highland fling on his hind legs like a dog possessed, It's maniacal, weird and eerie.*
>
> KILLER *shakes his head and turns back into a dog.*

High as a fuckin' kite off my fuckin' face.

Bitches!

WOMAN: Gotta get
   To ridge
   To space

KILLER: Couldn't fuckin' help myself.

WOMAN: To breathe
   To get away

KILLER: Those fucking bitches!

WOMAN: Dingo, you okay?

KILLER: Rrrrraaorrrrrrrr!

> WOMAN *grabs* DINGO, *almost dragging her, and they exit.*
>
> KILLER DOG LOST *exits in pursuit of* WOMAN *and* DINGO.

SCENE EIGHT

WOMAN *crashes through country, struggling with her load of swaddled dead* DOG, *pack, gun, skins, billy et cetera. Dragging/carrying injured* DINGO ...

As she runs it darkens, storm clouds are rolling in.

Images scroll past, reminiscent of Scene Six, but this time it is a nightmare. A frightening 'woman's-eye view' of her chase through the country. It might be almost abstract in places, hard to make sense of for both audience and WOMAN. WOMAN *is obsessed.*

Soundscape echoes all around, freaky, becoming distorted, including ...

Sounds of footsteps, running, crashing through trees and plants.

WOMAN*'s rough hard breathing.*
Distant growls of KILLER DOG LOST.
Gunshots.
And, strangely, the ghostly wail of bagpipes, barely discernible.
Mist envelopes them.
The bagpipes become louder.

WOMAN: Up
  my pace
  to match
  my pulse.

  Gotta

  I know you're there!

  You mongrel

  Don't like

  Watched.
  Stalked
  Wild thing
  out there
  somewhere.
  Near.

  Get away!

  Get away from me!

  I've got you, Dingo!

  Gotta get

  heart pounds

  Gotta

  Gun

  Gotta

  Load

You won't get me!

Dingo!

I've got nothing.
Wake up!
No shot! No ammo!

Runnnnn!

Dingo?!
Help!
I can't …
DINGO: Listen to them, Woman.
WOMAN: Who?
DINGO: They yowl to you.
WOMAN: No!
    My boots wet.
DINGO: You who barged on in.
WOMAN: Pack wet.
DINGO: Without the smarts to stop.
WOMAN: Cold, so cold.
DINGO: Not looking …
WOMAN: … Keep moving.
DINGO: To see, hear the patterns.
WOMAN: Wet drips down my trousers wet.
DINGO: And take heed.
WOMAN: Cold needles in my back wet.
DINGO: And you crash through us all.
WOMAN: It wasn't meant to be like this.
DINGO: But I will stay …
WOMAN: He's still coming.
    Keep moving.
    Wrap gun in tarp.
    Keep moving.
    Shoulders aching.
    So heavy, you weigh a tonne.
    Left foot.
    Keep moving.

Right foot.
Still coming.
Tarp keeps flapping open.
Keeps fuckin' flapping and I've got to keep it dry keep Mum's gun
dry tuck that fuckin' corner tuck that fuckin' tuckin' corner in around
through fingers cold too cold and wet too wet.
Wasn't meant to be like this.
Scramble onto ridge higher
left foot
I'm sorry, Dog,
right foot
I'm sorry
left foot
tall trees gone
heave over boulders
I'm sorry needles shiver
higher
neck
spasm
higher
needles shiver
spasm
head
boulders
right foot
pounds
left foot
pounds—

Arrrggghhhhh!

Ankle!
DINGO: Ohhhhwwwww!
WOMAN: Ankle explodes
    rocks buckle crumble collapse fold roll
    crash
    gun
    protect gun

Dingo
protect Dingo
tumble release
tumble release
Dingo
too big
face down face down
gasp
arms where arms?
Dog where Dog?
Mum's gun?
Skins where skins?
Pinned
face down
neck pressed dead weight no arch no lift
can't
gasp
hot
can't
gasp
pressed held pain cold

can't

cold

can't …

   WOMAN *loses consciousness.* DINGO *slowly and painfully stirs.*

DINGO: You crash in and tear us apart,
   Like insatiable beasts ripping flesh from bones.
   And you dare to call us wild?

   Wild never was until you came.
   We had our ways from forever.
   How to live.
   How to kill.
   How to share.
   And now you have to see.
      Silence.

Snow gently starts to fall.

DINGO *sniffs* WOMAN. *Pisses on the ground around her. Lies beside her awhiles.*

DINGO *gets up, walks around, sniffing* WOMAN *again.*

Wake up!

Woman.

Get up.

DINGO *tries to push* WOMAN *upright with her nose.*

Come on, Woman. Too cold to sleep here now.

Wake up!
Wake up!
Wake up!

Here … Here …

Come now …

DINGO *drags skins away from* WOMAN. *Nudges* WOMAN *with her muzzle, tries to roll her over.*

Wake up. Wake up, my little one …

DINGO *licks* WOMAN, *who stirs slightly.*

Come on now.

DINGO *snuggles up to* WOMAN*'s face, and offers her nipples.*

WOMAN *instinctively accepts. She is dangerously thirsty.*

Here, my little one.
You drink
What my own dead babies can't.

I need you …

I need you to see.

Slowly WOMAN *wakes.* DINGO *gently backs a little away.*

They look into each other's eyes for some time while WOMAN *regains her presence, unsettled, unsure.*

WOMAN: Where's the dog?

DINGO: Which one?

WOMAN: The dog, the dog … you know the one … that mongrel killer …

DINGO: There's a few of those in this story …

WOMAN: Dog! I just need a dog …

>   WOMAN *breaks down and sobs.*

DINGO: Yes. You do …

>   Those killers are out there still.
>   Maybe always.

>>   DINGO *silently gestures to show* WOMAN *that there is no live dog close by …*

>   But I'm here.

WOMAN: I'm frightened …

DINGO: And it's cold and there's wilder weather on its way …

WOMAN: Thank you … for …

DINGO: … and it's going to be a rough night … and neither of us are in good shape …

WOMAN: No …

>   Will you let me see?

DINGO: What?

WOMAN: Those wounds …?

>   He was a monster.

DINGO: Who do you think you are?

WOMAN: I could …

>   Maybe? …

>   Help?

DINGO: Are you my mother?

>   Do you have her healing tongue?
>   Could you lick lick lick like her?
>   Rolling over my ripped skin,
>   cleaning out the muck?
>   Her saliva medicine to any infection?

WOMAN: No.

>   I'm not.
>   But … if I see …?
>   Maybe? … (I can help—?)

DINGO: Are you my little family?
    Do you have their soothing bodies?
    Could you wrap yourself around me
    all our ridges and gullies fitting together
    like ancient tectonic plates
    so we breathe as one?
WOMAN: No.
DINGO: No. Indeed.
WOMAN: Just trying …
DINGO: Well …
WOMAN: Where are we? Where are those monsters?
    We're not safe.
DINGO: We can't go any higher.
WOMAN: Look at you.
DINGO: We're at the pinnacle.
    Where the dreaming begins and ends.
    Where the past, present and future collide.
    Where the real and unreal is all possible.

    Pause.

WOMAN: What do we do now …?
DINGO: Listen.

    WOMAN *struggles to understand. The sounds of chanting and
    clapsticks rise up from the lakes.*

WOMAN: What?
    To what?
DINGO: To the people.
    The women at the lakes

    And the greedy men who got turned into stone.

    Down there!

    The haunting bagpipes return.

WOMAN: Oh look, the farm!
    Mum and Dad will be worried sick.

    There's the Patterson Estate.

    *The distorted sounds of sheep add to the bagpipes, with increasing
    volume. The sound is swirling, surrounding audience and stage.*

DINGO: Brabralung Country

WOMAN: The Austins'.

DINGO: Brabralung Country

WOMAN: The Clarkes'.

DINGO: Brabralung Country

WOMAN: Oh my …

Mum's got the fire on!

DINGO: Old Money.

Holding on for dear life.

WOMAN: She'll be cooking scones or pickling.

And worrying where I am …

DINGO: Just sit at a place long enough and then it's yours? Don't even have to mark your scent? Or fight for it? Or did you …?

WOMAN: That is our farm!

DINGO *points out some landmarks.*

DINGO: Oh, look! There's Butcher's Creek, Boney Point, Skull Creek, Nigger's Leap …

WOMAN: Shut up! Shut up! Shut up!

DINGO: Old Angus McMillan , the '*discoverer* of Gippsland', and his Brigade of Merry Men.

You shoulda heard them play those bagpipes.

WOMAN: No!

DINGO: Frightened the shit out of us!

Dingoes *and* men.

A real fucking highland fling!

WOMAN: Go away!

DINGO: Rampaged through here like a monster.

Killing and clearing.

Snapping and biting.

WOMAN: Stop it!

DINGO: We saw it!

For ten years they fought the 'Black War'.

WOMAN: What war?!

DINGO: They stood their ground.

WOMAN: We've broken our backs on that farm!

DINGO: The Brabralung men speared the sheep and Angus McMillan shot the men!

And the women and children.

Us dingoes scattered too!

WOMAN: We've worked that land.

DINGO: And the Brabralung circle around the settlers' hut.

WOMAN: My grandfather …

DINGO: That man's kidnapped one of their women, see?

WOMAN: … and his father …

DINGO: Scared shitless in the bush with the Brabralung men circling, spears at the ready.

WOMAN: … and his father …

DINGO: He's surrounded the hut with hot coals to burn bare feet. Woman's chained up in the hut.

WOMAN: … and his father before them.

DINGO: And the Brabralung men lured him out and speared him!

WOMAN: No!

DINGO: And speared him and speared him and speared him!

WOMAN: Get away from me!

DINGO: That fulla had so many spears in his body, he couldn't fall down!

Died standing up!

WOMAN: Get away!

DINGO: Then the reprisals.

WOMAN: Stop!

DINGO: See the bend of that creek?

WOMAN: That's our farm, that's our swimming hole.

DINGO: With the cliff on the other side.

WOMAN: My pa taught me how to swim in that swimming hole.

DINGO: Snuck up on the women's camp around lunchtime. Chased them into the waterhole with their guns firing. The women held their children under the water until they had to come up for air. They couldn't get to the other side on account of the cliffs. They were trapped, see.

Popped them off. One by one. Bang. Bang. Bang. Thirty-six women and children. The water ran red. On your beloved land.

Pause.

WOMAN *cries.*

Like I knew she would.

WOMAN: Why didn't they tell me?!

DINGO: And the people and dingoes scattered.

But we're coming back!

WOMAN: I wanna go home. I have to go home!

DINGO: It was their home. Always was …

WOMAN: I … can't … breathe …

Gotta … / get home …

DINGO: Blood. Red blood. We saw it. We smelt it.

> DINGO *and* WOMAN *stare into each other's eyes intently.*

WOMAN: Who are you? What are you? You're not me!

Stop! Stop!

Stop talking to me!

You're a dog!

A fucking dog!

DINGO: And then you'll start all over again.

Because that's what you do.

WOMAN: What do you want?!

DINGO: Just leave.

Leave us alone.

Fuck off!

> *Sound out.*

> *Silence.*

> DINGO *drags herself away and curls herself into a deathbed. They both lie spent, exhausted, dying physically and metaphorically.* WOMAN *gets up and sees that* DINGO *is bleeding out.*

WOMAN: We're dying up here.

DINGO: Yes. We are.

WOMAN: You're bleeding! Let me look.

DINGO: Like a red river. Going now.

WOMAN: No! No! You can't!

DINGO: A one-hundred-dollar skin. Cash me in.

A mere pinprick in the sky.

WOMAN: No! You can't!

No!

Please …

Pause.

DINGO: Fucking …

Beautiful …

> DINGO *closes her eyes. The Dreaming takes her.*
>
> WOMAN *holds* DINGO *and sobs.*

WOMAN: Like she knew I would.

> WOMAN *weeps and howls and howls and howls to the moon.*
>
> *Distant dingoes join in and pay homage.*
>
> *A little* DINGO PUP, *shivering at the base of a tree, comes into view.*
>
> *The howling stops.*

Hey …

What?

Little dingo pup?

Where's your …?

You're shivering, little one …

Come here …

> *She goes to pick up* PUP. PUP *growls and nips her. Drawing blood.*

Ouch! I'm not like them.

> *Pause.*
>
> *Neither of them move.*

What's your name?
Hello? Hello?

> PUP *whimpers.*

Are you hurt?

> *She moves towards* PUP. PUP *skitters and snarls, backs away from her. They hold eye contact*

Hey? What's wrong?

I won't hurt you.

I'm not going any further.

Hello? Hello?

Tell me a story.

    PUP *moves further away.*

Talk to me!

    PUP *backs further away.*

Hello?

Tell me what I have to do?

I wasn't there, I'm just the daughter of a daughter of a daughter …

I'm sorry …

    PUP *backs away further and is disappearing into the bush.*

Come back!

Come back, little one!

Talk to me!

Come back!

Don't go!

    PUP *has melted back into the landscape.*

    WOMAN *cannot stand. She stands and falls. Stands and falls. She sobs and whimpers.*

    She turns into stone.

    Lights fade to black.

    The lone sound of the heartbeat of an agitated female.

THE END

GRIFFIN THEATRE COMPANY PRESENTS
IN ASSOCIATION WITH FORCE MAJEURE

GRIFFIN
THEATRE
COMPANY

DOGGED

BY ANDREA JAMES
& CATHERINE RYAN

30 APRIL – 5 JUNE 2021
SBW STABLES THEATRE

DIRECTOR
DECLAN GREENE

ASSOCIATE DIRECTOR
DANIELLE MICICH

MOVEMENT DIRECTOR
KIRK PAGE

SET CO-DESIGNER AND
COSTUME DESIGNER
RENÉE MULDER

SET CO-DESIGNER &
MURAL ARTIST
PETER WAPLES-CROWE

LIGHTING DESIGNER
VERITY HAMPSON

SOUND & COMPOSITION
STEVE TOULMIN

STAGE MANAGER
ELLA GRIFFIN

ASSISTANT STAGE MANAGER
NICOLA STAVAR

ASSOCIATE MURAL ARTIST
JESSICA JOHNSON

WITH
**BLAZEY BEST
SANDY GREENWOOD
ANTHONY YANGOYAN**

pported by
ffin's Production Partner program

Government partners

ODUCTION
ARTNER

force
majeure

NSW
GOVERNMENT

Australian Government

Australia
Council
for the Arts

Griffin acknowledges the generosity of the Seaborn,
Broughton & Walford Foundation in allowing it the use of the
SBW Stables Theatre rent free, less outgoings, since 1986.

PLAYWRIGHTS' NOTE

Hi. This is Cath. Andrea suggested, and I agreed, that I would start this note about *Dogged*. And that's a teeny tiny taste of the wondrous and energising co-writing process we continue to make for ourselves. A question here, an offer there, consideration, discussion, respect, decision.

Like when I try to tell any story, I find it hard to know where this one starts.

Does *Dogged* start in 2018, when I hopefully asked Andrea, who had directed an earlier Development Workshop, to join me in creating it anew? Or was it in 2012, when I was captivated and troubled by the complexities of the Victorian government's hunting bounty on the skin of a "wild" dog, Dingo or fox—a response to the challenges faced by farmers whose sheep were being increasingly killed... And the photo of a young white farming woman proudly displaying her skins. Our story also has a beginning in the 1840s, when the first white men invaded Gunaikurnai Country over the mountains. And on January 26, 1788, and around 5,000 years before that, when Dingoes are thought to have arrived on this continent now known as Australia. And before that too... ever asking "How do we living beings relate with each other and land?".

I feel like life is a multi-dimensional web of stories, spinning eternal beginnings and never-endings: interconnecting, conflicting, supporting, echoing, blocking and flowing. I have massive heartfelt thanks and respect to Andrea for her trust, generosity, clarity, great theatrical storytelling skills and wisdom as we weave our threads together here. And to Griffin for welcoming us dogs.

Hi. Andrea here, breezing into Cath's slipstream. When Cath invited me to bring a Gunaikurnai perspective to her story, I initially knocked her back. Her writing was so rich and poetic, I didn't want to ruin its beauty by bringing a different writing style to the table. I felt crude and clunky compared to Cath's intelligent verse. But Cath persisted, and I came to understand that I had something to add to her intriguing story and characters. There was such vividness and shock in her poetry, but Cath wasn't precious about her work. So together, we blew up her play and let the pieces land. I was all about THE ACTION and Cath was all about THE FEELINGS and she encouraged me to dig deeper and to feel—the hard stuff and the good stuff. I also introduced a shitload of swear words into the play and became the custodian of the Dingo character; Cath became the custodian of the Woman and Dog characters. Together, we formed a deeper connection with my Grandmother's Country and with each other. Writing, for me, is a deeply cultural act—it's literally about survival. It connects me to my People and Country and is intended for generations to come, and I am so pleased that Cath came along for that wild ride too.

We yarned, we followed our noses, and we met with people and family who knew of Dingoes and my Grandmother's Country. Reconnecting back to that place was an essential starting point. How liberating it was to see my Grandmother's Country and people through the eyes of a Dingo. Our interdependent and graceful connection with Dingoes is precious but has also been under threat. For us mob, the distinctions between animals, humans and landforms are nebulous. We do not categorise or put ourselves above others. There is an interconnectedness that has nurtured land and people for centuries.

Somehow all of these myriad thoughts, and Cath's initial creative spark, have forged a unified moral tale for today that hopefully sharpens your vision and softens your heart.

Like my forebears, there is much to learn from watching Country and her totemic animals and birds with intent.

Andrea James & Catherine Ryan
Co-Writers

We pay our respects to the Gunaikurnai on whose land this play is set. Special thanks to our cultural consultants Ron Murray, Tim Paton and Glenys Watts. Thanks to dramaturg Peter Matheson and Playwriting Australia for their crucial roles in the play's development. And to Arnum Endean, Daydd Kelly, Xanthe Ryan, Erik-dog and Lucy-dog, for being with us all the way. And all the other dingoes, dogs and people who shared their selves and stories with us, especially Wandi.

DIRECTOR'S NOTE

On first reading, *Dogged* struck me as a work of 21st century Australian Gothic horror. But my biggest chill came after I turned the final page. Spellbound and overwhelmed, I sat down at my computer to get some more context for the play. Even though I grew up on Gunaikurnai Land, where *Dogged* is set, I knew little about the colonial history of the area—and even less about its Blak history. I started by Googling 'Angus McMillan'—the Scottish pastoralist whose horrifying massacres are described in the play. And to my shock and shame, I found that I had grown up in an electorate named after him: the Division of McMillan. Our family home, our street, our town—all party to a bureaucratic honouring of this man, and the blood he had shed in the theft of land and waters. In 2018, the electorate was quietly re-named (after a different white guy—Sir John Monash). But across the state of Victoria—in Sale, Stratford, Heyfield, Yarram, Omeo, Lucknow—markers and statues remain, memorialising McMillan as the Discoverer of Gippsland.

I don't actually know that Andrea and Cath would describe Dogged as "Australian Gothic". Maybe this over-simplifies what is also an innovative, intuitive, and muscular piece of experimental playwriting. But as an obsessive lover of *Wake In Fright*, *Picnic at Hanging Rock, The Proposition*—I can't help but see the play in this context. Like all genres, Australian Gothic has its clichés. We think of hoop skirts and starched priest collars against the red dirt of the outback. We think of white schoolgirls in frilly dresses lost in the bush. But Anna Valdine Clemens more closely describes the Gothic genre as the "*return of the repressed*." She writes: "*Some entity, knowledge, emotion, or feeling*" which has been "*held at bay because it threatens the established order of things, develops a cumulative energy that demands its release*".

To my mind, this describes *Dogged* precisely. The repressed history of McMillan's crimes bubble beneath the surface of the play. When they finally burst through, it is as if the text itself cracks open. In *Dogged's* opening scenes, Andrea and Cath promise us a tense thriller: a stand-off between a woman and a dingo poised at the end of a gun... Before they lead us, hand-in-hand, into a swirling fog of poetry, blurred realities, and visions of monstrous violence.

In our first meeting about *Dogged*, Andrea described the play to me as a collaboration between First Nations and Settler artists—to negotiate ideas of territory, guilt, and culpability. Alongside Cath, I am indebted to Andrea's wisdom and guidance over the process of preparing this production, and to collaborators Peter Waples-Crowe, Kirk Page, and Sandy Greenwood. To be entrusted with the first production of this play is an honour, and a responsibility I do not take lightly.

Declan Greene
Director

BIOGRAPHIES

ANDREA JAMES
CO-WRITER

Andrea James is a Yorta Yorta/Gunaikurnai woman and a graduate of the Victorian College of the Arts. She makes work that reflects her identity, sharing historical and contemporary stories of Aboriginal experiences within sharp contemporary theatrical language and form. Andrea is an experienced collaborator, playwright, producer and director. She was a recipient of British Council's Accelerate Program for Aboriginal Art Leaders in 2013 and was awarded an Arts NSW Aboriginal Arts Fellowship. She has produced for Carriageworks, Blacktown Arts Centre and Urban Theatre Projects. She was Artistic Director of Melbourne Workers Theatre 2001-2008 where she is best known for her play *Yanagai! Yanagai!*. Her playwriting credits include: as Co-Writer: for ILBIJERRI Theatre Company/La Mama: *Coranderrk* (with Giordano Nanni); for Arthur/Theatre Works: *Bright World* (with Elise Hearst); and as Playwright: for Urban Theatre Projects: *Blacktown Angels* (part of *Home Country*); for JUTE Theatre: *Bukal*; and for Moogahlin Performing Arts Projects: *Winyanboga Yurringa* (which was remounted at Belvoir in 2019). Her works have shown throughout Australia, in the UK, Paris and New York. She is currently a Writer-In-Residence at Melbourne Theatre Company developing *The Black Woman of Gippsland* from her grandmother's country. Her play, *Sunshine Super Girl*, about Wiradjuri tennis superstar Evonne Goolagong-Cawley, was produced by Performing Lines and premiered in Griffith before travelling to Sydney Festival. Andrea is Griffin's Associate Artist.

CATHERINE RYAN
CO-WRITER

A VCA graduate Animateur, Catherine's practice is inspired by questions about interconnectedness, empathy, the dynamics of relationships and power, and the spaces and obstacles between us. Of Anglo-Irish settler/invader heritage, she gratefully lives on unceded Dja Dja Wurrung country (Central Victoria). In 2001, she co-founded Castlemaine's Barking Owl Theatre, co-creating many original and community-based works in their eight years of activity. In 2009, Catherine won an AWGIE for Best Radio Adaptation for *Aurora Calling: The Results of a Joint Observation*, which was then the Australian nominee in its category at the Prix Italia International Media Awards. Her work has also won a George Fairfax Award (*Precipice*) and two Inscription Awards (*Getting Away From It All, Precipice*), along with several other national (Patrick White, Griffin and Hal Porter Short Story Awards) and international (Perishable Theatre International Women's Playwright) shortlistings. She has been a Resident Playwright at Griffin, an Affiliate Writer at the Melbourne Theatre Company, and has been commissioned by ABC Radio National and Malthouse Theatre. She is also a dramaturg for stage and documentary film. Catherine's work has appeared at Griffin, the Castlemaine State Festival, La Mama Theatre, on ABC Radio National, and in *Overland* and *Antipodes* journals.

DECLAN GREENE
DIRECTOR

Declan is the Artistic Director of Griffin Theatre Company, and works as a playwright, dramaturg and director. As Director, his credits include: for Griffin: *Green Park*; for Malthouse Theatre: *Wake in Fright*; for Malthouse Theatre and Sydney Theatre Company: *Blackie Blackie Brown*; for Sydney Theatre Company: *Hamlet: Prince of Skidmark*; for ZLMD Shakespeare Company: *Conviction*. As Playwright, his work includes *Eight Gigabytes of Hardcore Pornography*, *The Homosexuals, or 'Faggots'*, *Melancholia*, *Moth*, and *Pompeii L.A.* Declan co-founded queer experimental theatre company Sisters Grimm with Ash Flanders in 2006, and has directed and co-created all their productions to date, including: for Griffin Independent and Theatre Works: *Summertime in the Garden of Eden*; for Malthouse Theatre and Sydney Theatre Company: *Calpurnia Descending*; for Melbourne Theatre Company: *Lilith: The Jungle Girl*; and for Sydney Theatre Company: *Little Mercy*. He was previously Resident Artist at Malthouse Theatre.

DANIELLE MICICH
ASSOCIATE DIRECTOR

Danielle Micich is a choreographer, director, intimacy coordinator and performer of dance theatre. She is currently Artistic Director of Force Majeure based at Carriageworks in Sydney. Danielle's contributes to making new Australian work through storytelling that reaches audiences by exploring themes and issues relevant to contemporary culture; reflecting, embracing and challenging community attitudes and ideals. Danielle makes new work for festivals, theatre productions, opera and film, alongside site-specific and community work. After graduating from the Victorian College of the Arts and relocating to Perth as a company dancer for 2 Dance Plus, she was appointed Artistic Director of STEPS Youth Dance Company. Her independent work extends nationally and internationally, working with companies such as Barking Gecko Theatre Company, Belvoir, Bell Shakespeare, Black Swan State Theatre Company, Monkey Baa Theatre, Night Train Productions, Perth Theatre Company, Pinchgut Opera, Sydney Theatre Company, Steamworks Arts Productions, and internationally at Dwhani Dance Company (India).

KIRK PAGE
MOVEMENT DIRECTOR

A descendant of the Mulandjali clan in South East Queensland, Kirk is a movement consultant, actor, writer and body-centred artist working in the performing arts and theatre sector across disciplines. Widely acclaimed for his physical theatre, aerial and dance work, Kirk has appeared in productions across the country and toured internationally throughout his career with companies such as Bangarra Dance Theatre and Legs on the Wall. From 2016 to 2019, Kirk was the Associate Artistic Director at the Northern Rivers Performing Arts Company (NORPA) in Lismore, NSW, creating works and programs engaging with First Nations youth and the local arts community. Kirk's theatre credits include: as Actor: for Back Row Productions: *Priscilla, Queen of the Desert*; for Black Swan State Theatre Company: *Corrguation Road*; for Malthouse Theatre: *One Night the Moon*; for Sydney Theatre Company: *The Sunshine Club*; as Movement Director: for NORPA: *Dreamland*; and as Director: for NORPA: *Djurra*; for NORPA/Beyond Empathy: *Horse's Mouth*. On screen, Kirk has appeared in the ABC television series *Redfern Now* and *Mystery Road*. As Movement Director, Kirk has worked on the film *Bran Nue Dae*, and ABC TV's *My Place*.

RENÉE MULDER
SET CO-DESIGNER AND COSTUME DESIGNER

Renée is an award-winning set and costume designer and Design Director at Queensland Theatre. Her theatre design credits include: for Griffin: *The Bleeding Tree*, *The Boys*, *Prima Facie*, *Superheroes*; for Griffin Independent: *The Pigeons*; for Griffin and La Boite: *A Hoax*; for Griffin and Queensland Theatre: *Rice*; for Bell Shakespeare: *Romeo and Juliet*; for La Boite: *As You Like It*, *Ruben Guthrie*, *I Love You, Bro*; for Melbourne Theatre Company: *Arbus and West*, *Home, I'm Darling*; for Queensland Theatre: *An Octoroon*, *Fat Pig*, *Mouthpiece*, *Nearer the Gods*, *Sacre Bleu!*; for Sydney Theatre Company: *Actor on a Box: The Luck Child*, *Banging Denmark*, *Battle of Waterloo*, *The Beauty Queen of Leenane*, *Black is the New White*, *Dance Better at Parties*, *Hamlet: Prince of Skidmark*, *In a Heart Beat*, *The Long Way Home, Mariage Blanc*, *Mrs Warren's Profession*, *Orlando*, *Perplex*, *The Splinter*, *The Torrents*; for Sydney Theatre Company and Queensland Theatre: *The Effect, Triple X*; and for Theatre Forward: *The Sneeze*. As Costume Designer, her credits include: for Sydney Theatre Company: *Children of the Sun*, *Chimerica*, *Endgame*, *The Harp in the South Part One and Part Two*, *Playing Beatie Bow*, *Saint Joan*, *Top Girls*; for Sydney Theatre Company and State Theatre Company of South Australia: *Vere (Faith)*. As Set Designer, her credits include: for Sydney Theatre Company and La Boite: *Edward Gant's Amazing Feats of Loneliness*. As Associate Designer, her credits include: for Sydney Theatre Company: *Cyrano de Bergerac*. Renée's film credits include, as Co-Production Designer: *A Parachute Falling in Siberia*; and as part of the armour art department: *The Chronicles of Narnia: The Voyage of the Dawn Treader*. Renée was Sydney Theatre Company's Resident Designer from 2012-2014, and was a member of Queensland Theatre's National Artistic Team from 2016-2017. She is a graduate of NIDA and Queensland College of Art.

PETER WAPLES-CROWE
SET CO-DESIGNER & MURAL ARTIST

Peter Waples-Crowe is a Ngarigo artist living in Melbourne. His intersecting experiences as an Aboriginal person and his work with community health and arts organisations give him a unique perspective as an artist and community cultural development worker. Peter creates bold, colourful work that explores the representation of Aboriginal people in popular culture, often referencing the Dingo as a totemic figure and an analogy for queer, outsider Mob. Peter's practice also consists of reworking of the colonial images from books and galleries print collections; diffracting the colonisers view of Aboriginal people with the mercurial wit of the constantly shifting negotiations of queer and black identities. Peter has been a multiple finalist for the National Aboriginal and Torres Strait Islander Art Awards, the Victorian Indigenous Art Award, and has received the three major awards throughout its ten year history. In 2019, Peter was awarded the Melbourne LGBTI Community GLOBE Artist of the Year Award, won the 2D Metro Tunnel Prize at the Koorie Art Show, completed the Leadership Victoria LGBTIQ Leadership program and was featured in a short documentary called *insideOUT* that screened in *Our Stories* on NITV in December.

VERITY HAMPSON
LIGHTING DESIGNER

Verity is a multi-award-winning lighting and projection designer who has designed over 130 productions, working with some of Australia's leading directors and choreographers. For theatre, Verity's designs include: for Griffin: *A Strategic Plan*, *And No More Shall We Part*, *Angela's Kitchen*, *Beached*, *The Bleeding Tree*, *The Boys*, *The Bull*, *The Moon and the Coronet of Stars*, *Dealing With Clair*, *The Floating World*, *Superheroes*, *This Year's Ashes*, *The Turquoise Elephant*; for Griffin Independent: *The Brothers Size*, *The Cold Child*, *Crestfall*, *Family Stories: Belgrade*, *Live Acts On Stage*, *Music*, *The New Electric Ballroom*, *References to Salvador Dali Make Me Hot*, *Way to Heaven*; for Griffin and Bell Shakespeare: *The Literati*; for Bell Shakespeare: *A Midsummer Night's Dream*, *Julius Caesar*, *Titus Andronicus*; for Belvoir: *An Enemy of the People*, *The Drover's Wife*, *Faith Healer*, *Winyanboga Yurringa*; for Ensemble: *Baby Doll*, *Fully Committed*; for Malthouse Theatre: *Wake In Fright*; for Queensland Theatre: *Death of a Salesman*; and for Sydney Theatre Company: *Blackie Blackie Brown*, *Hamlet: Prince of Skidmark*, *Home, I'm Darling*, *Machinal*, *Little Mercy*. Verity is a recipient of the Mike Walsh Fellowship; three Sydney Theatre Awards; a Green Room Award; and an APDG Award for Best Lighting Design.

STEVE TOULMIN
COMPOSER AND SOUND DESIGNER

Steve's credits as Composer and/or Sound Designer include: for Griffin: *Beached*, *The Bleeding Tree*, *Feather in the Web*, *Gloria*, *Kill Climate Deniers*; for Griffin and La Boite: *A Hoax*; for Griffin and Malthouse Theatre: *The Homosexuals, or 'Faggots'*; for Bell Shakespeare: *Othello*, *Richard III*; for Belvoir: *20 Questions*, *44 Sex Acts in One Week*, *Barbara and the Camp Dogs*, *The Blind Giant is Dancing*, *Blue Wizard*, *Hir*, *Is This Thing On?*, *Ivanov*, *Jasper Jones*, *La Traviata*, *Scorched*, *The Seed*; for Ensemble Theatre: *Circle Mirror Transformation*, *Great Falls*, *Liberty Equality Fraternity*; for La Boite: *Hamlet*, *Julius Caesar*, *Tender Napalm*; for La Boite and Sydney Theatre Company: *Edward Gant's Amazing Feats of Loneliness*; for Michael Sieders Presents: *Porn. Cake*; for Queensland Theatre: *Switzerland*, *That Face*; for Strut & Fret: *Blanc De Blanc*, *Blanc de Blanc Encore*, *Fun House*, *Life*; for Sydney Festival: *All The Sex I've Ever Had*, *Maureen: Harbinger of Death*; and for Sydney Theatre Company: *A Flea in Her Ear*, *Black is the New White*, *Power Plays*, *Little Mercy*. Steve's credits within the independent sector include: *After All This*, *Me Pregnant!*, *Prehistoric*, *Queen of Wolves*, *Rommy*, *Trapture*; and his work in events includes the *EKKA Arena Spectacular* (2013-2015) and Papua New Guinea's 40th Year of Independence Celebrations.

ELLA GRIFFIN
STAGE MANAGER

Ella is a Sydney-based stage manager and graduate of the Bachelor of Fine Arts (Technical Theatre & Stage Management) at NIDA. Since graduating in 2018, Ella has had the pleasure of working for mainstage and commercial productions both in Sydney and internationally. As an Assistant Stage Manager, her credits include: for Griffin: *City of Gold*; for Bangarra Dance Theatre: *Spirit: A Retrospective* (2021 Regional Tour); for Belvoir: *Winyanboga Yurringa*; for Sydney Theatre Company: *Mary Stuart*, *The Picture of Dorian Gray* (Swing), *Wonnangatta* (Swing). As Stage Manager, Ella has worked on *Trestle*, a new work development for Legs On The Wall. Internationally, in 2020 Ella worked in both the UK and Russia as Assistant Stage Manager on *Jean Paul Gaultier: Fashion Freak Show*, a musical produced by RGM Productions. Beyond stage management, Ella has worked across a variety of events in Sydney, as an Assistant Event Coordinator for Sydney Festival 2021 across the Seymour Centre program, as well as in various roles on the Rob Guest Endowment, Helpmann Awards, and Griffin's *Scratch* and *The Lysicrates Prize*. Ella is delighted to be making her mainstage debut as Stage Manager for *Dogged*.

NICOLA STAVAR
ASSISTANT STAGE MANAGER

In recent years, Nicola has been the Assistant Stage Manager on a number of productions with Sydney Theatre Company, including: *Blackie Blackie Brown*, *Going Down* and *The Real Thing*. Other ASM credits include: for Sydney Opera House and The Works: *The Illusionists: Direct from Broadway*; for Storyboard Entertainment: *Barnum: The Circus Musical*; and most recently, the LPD Productions and Sydney Opera House production of *RENT*. Nicola is a graduate of the Queensland University of Technology.

BLAZEY BEST
WOMAN

One of Australia's most versatile and accomplished actresses, Blazey Best has an extensive list of performing credits and was most recently seen in Belvoir's *My Brilliant Career*. Previous credits incude: for Griffin: *Strange Attractor* (for which she received a Sydney Theatre Award Nomination for Best Supporting Actress); for Belvoir: *Death of a Salesman*, *Medea*, *Ivanov*, *Nora*, *Miss Julie*, *The Wild Duck* (International Tour); for Luckiest Productions: *Gypsy*, *Miracle City*, *Only Heaven Knows*; for Sydney Theatre Company: *Arcadia*, *Summer Rain*, *Travesties*, *Troupers*, *Wharf Revue*; for Bell Shakespeare: *The Comedy of Errors* (National and UK Tour), *Much Ado About Nothing*, *Richard lll*, *Troilus + Cressida*, *The Servant of Two Masters*, *The War of the Roses*; for Michael Coppel: *Fawlty Towers*; for Showtune Productions: *Hedwig and the Angry Inch*; for Luna Hare: *B-Girl*; and for Sydney and Adelaide Festivals: *The Iliad Out Loud*. In film, Blazey has appeared in *Powder Burn*, Brendan Cowell's *Ruben Guthrie*, *Stealth*, *Ten Empty* and *West*. Her recent work in television includes: for ABC: *Janet King*, *Rake*, and for Seven Network: *A Place to Call Home*, *Between Two Worlds*, *Home and Away*, *The Killing Field*. Blazey has won Sydney Theatre Awards for her performances in *Ivanov*, *Miracle City* and *Medea*.

SANDY GREENWOOD
DINGO

Sandy is a First Nations actor and playwright from the Dunghutti, Gumbaynggirr and Bundjalung tribes of Australia. She has a Bachelor of Fine Arts (Drama, Theatre Studies), Honours, from the Queensland University of Technology, as well as having trained at Atlantic Acting School in New York City, and The Groundlings in Los Angeles. Sandy has performed with a number of Australia's leading theatre companies, including: for Melbourne Theatre Company: *First Stage*; for Sydney Theatre Company: *Stolen*, *Taboo*; and several leading roles for ILBIJERRI Theatre Company. Sandy has also performed on the international stage at Seattle Children's Theatre Company in *Afternoon of the Elves*. On screen, she has appeared in the US blockbuster *Killer Elite* alongside Robert de Niro, for which she received a Deadly Award nomination for Indigenous Actor of the Year. She was also the lead in the feature film *Little Black Dress*. Her short film credits include: *A Metamorphosis Engineered*, *All is Forgiven*, *Blind Date*, *Candy Cravings*, *Crossing*, *Flame of the West*, *Love Crossed*, *The Shoe Whisperer*. Sandy's television appearances include *Home and Away* and *Takoyaki City*. Sandy was also a producer's attachment on *Miss Fisher's Murder Mysteries*. In Australia, Sandy is perhaps best known for her critically-acclaimed one-woman show, *Matriarch*, for which she was recognised with a Green Room Award in 2019 for Best Performer, Independent Theatre.

ANTHONY YANGOYAN
DOG

Anthony was born in Sydney, Australia where he grew up in Sydney's inner west. Anthony relocated to Melbourne where he graduated with a Bachelor of Fine Arts (Acting) at the Victorian College of the Arts in 2019. Anthony's theatre credits include: for Breath & Bones Theatre Company: *DNA*; for Company Clan: *The Shape of Things*; and for VCA: *A View from the Bridge*, *The Cherry Orchard*, *The Comedy of Errors*, *DFLTLX*, *Mad Forest*. In 2019, Anthony co-wrote and performed in *Tiger Cage* at VCA's Discord 879 Festival. Anthony recently starred in the web series *Frank's Patch*. Anthony aims to create work that promotes inclusion and diversity within the theatre industry.

ABOUT GRIFFIN

Griffin is the only theatre company in the country entirely devoted to new Australian plays. Located in the historic SBW Stables Theatre, nestled in the heart of bustling Kings Cross, Griffin has been a permanent home for the exploration of Australian stories since 1978.

Many of this country's most beloved and celebrated artists started out on our stage—Cate Blanchett, Michael Gow, Alma De Groen, David Wenham, to name a few—and iconic Australian plays like The Boys, Holding the Man and City of Gold had their world premieres at Griffin, before going out to capture the national imagination. We are a theatre of first chances.

We are passionate about nurturing emerging artists. We help ambitious, bold, risk-taking and urgent Australian plays get from a page onto a stage. We tell the stories that will help us know who we are as a nation, and who we want to become.

Stories about us. Written by us. For us.

Griffin Theatre Company and the SBW Stables Theatre operate and tell stories on the unceded lands of the Gadigal of the Eora Nation. We acknowledge and honour Aboriginal and Torres Strait Islander people as the oldest continuous living culture on the planet, with more than 60,000 years of storytelling practice shaping and underpinning all aspects of Australian culture. It is a privilege that we do not take lightly: to work on this land, and to tell stories on its soil.

GRIFFIN THEATRE COMPANY
13 Craigend St
Kings Cross NSW 2011

02 9332 1052
info@griffintheatre.com.au
griffintheatre.com.au

SBW STABLES THEATRE
10 Nimrod St
Kings Cross NSW 2011

BOOKINGS
griffintheatre.com.au
02 9361 3817

GRIFFIN FAMILY

PATRON
Seaborn Broughton
& Walford Foundation

Griffin acknowledges the generosity of the Seaborn, Broughton & Walford Foundation in allowing it the use of the SBW Stables Theatre rent free, less outgoings, since 1986.

BOARD
Bruce Meagher (Chair)
Simon Burke AO
Julieanne Campbell
Helen Dai
Lyndell Droga
Tim Duggan
Declan Greene
Julia Pincus
Lenore Robertson
Simone Whetton
Meyne Wyatt

ARTISTIC
Artistic Director & CEO
Declan Greene

Associate Artistic Director
Tessa Leong

Associate Artist
Andrea James

Literary Associates
Julian Larnach
Poppy Tidswell

ADMINISTRATION
Executive Director
Julieanne Campbell

Associate Producer – Development
Frankie Greene

Associate Producer – Programming
Imogen Gardam

Associate Producer – Marketing
AJ Lamarque

Marketing Coordinator
Ang Collins

Marketing Assistant
Rebecca Abdel-Messih

Development Coordinator
Ell Katte

Program & Administration Coordinator
Whitney Richards

Strategic Insights Consultant
Peter O'Connell

PRODUCTION
Production Manager
Ryan Garreffa

Production Coordinator
Ally Moon

FINANCE
Finance Consultant
Tracey Whitby

Finance Manager
Kylie Richards

CUSTOMER RELATIONS
Box Office Manager
Dominic Scarf

Bar Manager
Grace Nye-Butler

Front of House
Patrick Boyle
Bridget Haberecht
Julian Larnach
Poppy Tidswell

Sustainability Coordinators
Ang Collins
Grace Nye-Butler

BRAND AND GRAPHIC DESIGN
Alphabet

COVER PHOTOGRAPHY
Brett Boardman

GRIFFIN DONORS

Income from Griffin activities covers less than 40% of our operating costs—leaving an ever-increasing gap for us to fill through government funding, sponsorship and the generosity of our individual supporters. Your support helps us bridge the gap and keep ticket prices affordable and our work at its best. To make a donation and a difference, contact Griffin on **9332 1052** or donate online at **griffintheatre.com.au**

COMPANY PATRONS
The Neilson Foundation

PRODUCTION PATRON
The Girgensohn Foundation

PROGRAM PATRONS

Griffin Ambassadors
Robertson Foundation

Griffin Studio Ensemble
Mary Ann Rolfe

Griffin Studio
Gil Appleton
Darin Cooper Foundation
Kiong Lee & Richard Funston
Rosemary Hannah &
Lynette Preston
Ken & Lilian Horler
Malcolm Robertson Foundation
Pip Rath & Wayne Lonergan
Mary Ann Rolfe
Geoff & Wendy Simpson OAM
Danielle Smith &
Sean Carmody
Walking up the Hill Foundation

Griffin Women's Initiative
Griffin Women's Initiative is supported by Creative Partnerships Australia through Plus1

Katrina Barter
Wendy Blacklock
Christy Boyce & Madeleine Beaumont
Laura Crennan
Lyndell Droga
Melinda Graham
Sherry Gregory
Antonia Haralambis
Ann Johnson
Roanne Knox
Julia Pincus
Ruth Ritchie
Lenore Robertson
Sonia Simich

Margie Sullivan
Deanne Weir
Simone Whetton

SEASON PATRONS
As a new writing theatre, we program a wide range of stories that reflect our time, place and the unique voice of contemporary Australia. To ensure that these stories continue to be told, Griffin needs the help of private support to bring strength, insight, candour and new and powerful visions to the stage. Our Production Partner program is vital to our continued artistic success.

PRODUCTION PARTNERS 2021
Dogged by **Andrea James & Catherine Ryan**
Lisa Barker & Don Russell
Darin Cooper Foundation
Robert Dick & Erin Shiel
Lyndell & Daniel Droga
Danny Gilbert AM &
Kathleen Gilbert
Rosemary Hannah &
Lynette Preston
Bruce Meagher & Greg Waters
Richard McHugh &
Kate Morgan
Julia Pincus & Ian Learmonth
Pip Rath & Wayne Lonergan

PRODUCTION PARTNERS 2020
Kindness **Matthew Whittet**
Darin Cooper Foundation

SEASON DONORS

Front Row Donors +$10,000
Anonymous (1)
Andrew Cameron AM &
Cathy Cameron
Darin Cooper Foundation

Robert Dick & Erin Shiel
Gordon & Marie Esden
Stephen Fitzgerald
Girgensohn Foundation
Ken & Lilian Horler
Malcolm Robertson Foundation
Sophie McCarthy &
Antony Green
Richard McHugh &
Kate Morgan
Bruce Meagher & Greg Waters
Peter & Dianne O'Connell
Rebel Penfold-Russell OAM
Julia Pincus & Ian Learmonth
Pip Rath & Wayne Lonergan
Ruth Ritchie
Robertson Foundation
Mary Ann Rolfe
The Sky Foundation
Merilyn Sleigh &
Raoul de Ferranti
The WeirAnderson Foundation
Kim Williams AM &
Catherine Dovey

**Main Stage Donor
$5,000 - $9,999**
Anonymous (1)
Antoinette Albert
Gil Appleton
Lisa Barker & Don Russell
Ellen Borda
Wendy Blacklock
Louise Christie
Bernard Coles
Lyndell & Daniel Droga
Danny Gilbert AM &
Kathleen Gilbert
Kiong Lee & Richard Funston
Lee Lewis & Brett Boardman
David Marr &
Sebastian Tesoriero
Catriona Morgan-Hunn
Don & Leslie Parsonage

GRIFFIN DONORS

Anthony Paull
Sue Procter
Geoff & Wendy Simpson OAM
Danielle Smith & Sean Carmody

Final Draft $2,000-$4,999
Gae Anderson
Baly Douglass Foundation
Helen Bauer & Helen Lynch AM
Marilyn & David Boyer
Iolanda Capodanno
Alan Colletti
Bryony & Tim Cox
Lachlan Edwards
Elizabeth Fullerton
Kathy Glass
Jocelyn Goyen
GRANTPIRRIE/privare
James Hartwright & Kerrin D'Arcy
Libby Higgin
Roanne & John Knox
Janet Manuell
Carina G. Martin
Philip Moore
John McCallum & Jenny Nicholls
John Mitchell
David Nguyen
Stuart Thomas
Tea Uglow
Richard Weinstein & Richard Benedict

Workshop Donor $1,000-$1,999
Anonymous (4)
Michael Barnes
Katrina Barter
Cherry & Peter Best
Christy Boyce & Madeleine Beaumont
Keith Bradley AM
Michael & Charmaine Bradley
Dr Bernadette Brennan
Jane Bridge
Corinne & Bryan
Stephen & Annabelle Burley
Susan Carleton
Adrian Christie
Sally Crawford
Laura Crennan
Nathan Croft & James White
Cris Croker & David West
Jane Curry

Timothy Davis
Carol Dettmann
T Dolland & S McComb
Sue and Jim Dominguez
Christine Dunstan
Bob Ernst
Ros & Paul Espie
Brian Everingham
John & Libby Fairfax
Rowena Falzon
Robyn Fortescue & Rosie Wagstaff
Jennifer Giles
Nicky Gluyas
Amelia Goff
Melinda Graham
Peter Gray & Helen Thwaites
Sherry Gregory
Antonia Haralambis
Kate Harrison
John Head
Danielle Hoareau
Mark Hopkinson & Michelle Opie
Susan Hyde
Ann Johnson
Deborah Jones
David & Adrienne Kitching
Jennifer Ledgar & Bob Lim
Richard & Elizabeth Longes
Chris Marrable & Kate Richardson
Elaine & Bill McLaughlin
Kent & Sandra McPhee
Joy Minter
Kate Mulvany
Jane Munro
Tommy Murphy
John Nethercoate
Ian Neuss & Penny Young
Patricia Novikoff
Ian Phipps
Martin Portus
Steve & Belinda Rankine
Judith & Frank Robertson
Sylvia Rosenblum
David & Dianne Russell
Sonia Simich
Jann Skinner
Geoffrey Starr

Leslie Stern
Robyn Stone
Adam Suckling & Pip McGuinness
Margie Sullivan
Peter Talbot
Mike Thompson
Sue Thomson
Daniel P. Tobin
Janet Wahlquist
Simone Whetton
Rosemary White
Paul & Jennifer Winch
Elizabeth Wing
Kathy Zeleny

Reading Donor $500-$999
Anonymous (3)
Brian Abel
Amity Alexander
Jes Andersen
Wendy Ashton
Robyn Ayres
Melissa Ball
Nikki Barrett
Phillip Black
Annie Bourke
Larry Boyd & Barbara Caine AM
Simon Burke AO
Marianne Bush
Bill Calcraft
Gaby Carney
Jane Christensen
Amanda Clark
Eloise Curry
Melita Daru
David Davies
Max Dingle
David Earp
Wendy Elder
Leonie Flannery
Peter Graves
Erica Gray
Stephanie & Andrew Harrison
Mary Holt
David Hoskins & Paul McKnight
Sylvia Hrovatin
Marian & Nabeel Ibrahim
David Jonas
Mira Joksovic
Susan J Kath

GRIFFIN DONORS

Susan Kippax
Maruschka Loupis
Anne Loveridge
Ian & Elizabeth MacDonald
Robert Marks
Rebecca Massey
Christopher McCabe
Wendy McCarthy AO
Patrick McIntyre
Nicole McKenna
Paula McLean
Daniela McMurdo
Dr Steve McNamara
Keith Miller
Stephen Mills
Neville Mitchell
William Peck
Carolyn Penfold
Judy Phillips
Malcolm Poole
Chris Puplick
Virginia Pursell
David Purves
Jennifer Rani
Alex-Oonagh Redmond
Chris Reed
Roslyn Renwick
Annabel Ritchie
Jonquil Ritter
Colleen Roche
Karen Rodgers & Bill Harris
Gemma Rygate
Rob & Rae Spence
Mary Stollery & Eric Dole
Catherine Sullivan & Alexandra Bowen
Pearl Tan & Priya Roy
Ariadne Vromen
Nancy Wahlquist
John Waters
William Zappa

First Draft Donor $200–$499
Anonymous (8)
Nicole Abadee & Rob Macfarlan
Priscilla Adey
Susan Ambler
Elizabeth Antonievich
Barbara Armitage
William Armitage

Chris Baker
Jan Barr
Grahame Best
Nicole Beyer
Edwina Birch
Rebecca Bourne Jones
Elizabeth Boyd
Shay Bristowe
Peter Brown
Dean Bryant & Mathew Frank
Wendy Buswell
Ruth Campbell
David Caulfield
Charlie Chan & Angela Catterns
Peter Chapman
Sue Clark
Amanda Connelly
Brendan Crotty & Darryl Toohey
Bryan Cutler
Joanne & Sue Dalton
Owen Davies
Dora Den Hengst
Susan Donnelly
Dr June Donsworth
Peter Duerden
Anna Duggan
Michele Dulcken
Kathy Esson
Elizabeth Evatt
Michael Eyers
Eamon Flack
Paul Fletcher
Helen Ford
Lee French
Matt Garrett
Sarah & Braith Gilchrist
Jock Given
Deane Golding
Thomas Gottlieb
Brenda Gottsche
Keith Gow
Hannah Grant
Virginia & Kieran Greene
Jo Grisard
Sue Hackett
Jennifer Hagan & Ron Blair
Glen Hamilton
Elizabeth Hanley
Carol Hargreaves
Raewyn Harlock

Grania Hickley
Lesley Hitchens
Stephanie Hui
Matthew Huxtable
C John Keightley
Maria Kelly
James Kelly & Beu Phuong
Catherine Kennedy
Penelope Latey
Antoinette Le Marchant
Peta Leemen
Caleb Lewis
Mark Lillis
Liz Locke
Norman Long
Dr Peter Louw
Carolyn Lowry
Anni MacDougall
Anne Mackarell
Guillermo Martin
Katrina Matthews
Louise McDonald
Edward McGuiness
Duncan McKay
Ellen McLoughlin
Ian McMillan
Sarah Miller
Bruce Milthorpe
Julia Mitchell
Catherine Moore
Pam Morris
Sarah Mort
Keith Moynihan
Mullinars Casting Consultants
Dian Neligan
Carolyn Newman
Gennie Nevinson & Vivian Manwaring
Sally Patten
Susheela Peres Da Costa
Peter Pezzutti
Meredith Phelps
Belinda Piggott & David Ojerholm
Marion Potts
Christopher Powell
Janelle Prescott
Andrew Pringle
Thelma Roach
In memory of Katherine

GRIFFIN DONORS

SPONSORS

Griffin would like to thank the following:

Government Supporters

Australian Government | Australia Council for the Arts

NSW GOVERNMENT

CITY OF SYDNEY

Patron

SBW Foundation

Production Patron

GIRGENSOHN FOUNDATION

Season Partner

NEILSON FOUNDATION

Creative Partners

alphabet.

Brett Boardman Photography

COPYRIGHTAGENCY CULTURAL FUND

MALCOLM ROBERTSON FOUNDATION

ROBERTSON FOUNDATION

Company Sponsors

bourke street bakery

Coopers

CURRENCY PRESS

FOUR PILLARS
PROUDLY EST. 2013
SMALL AUSTRALIAN DISTILLERY

MARQUE

MOPPITY

Rosenfeld, Kant & Co.
Business & Financial Solutions

SATURDAY PAPER

THE UNIVERSITY OF SYDNEY

Griffin Theatre Company is assisted by the Australian Government through the Australia Council, its arts funding and advisory body; and the NSW Government through Create NSW.

www.ingramcontent.com/pod-product-compliance
Lightning Source LLC
Chambersburg PA
CBHW050021090426
42734CB00021B/3359